Bulletin Boards and 3-D Showcases That Capture Them with Pizzazz

Volume 2

Bulletin Boards and 3-D Showcases

That Capture Them with Pizzazz

Volume 2

Karen Hawthorne
and
Jane E. Gibson

Illustrated by Jane E. Gibson

2002
Teacher Ideas Press
Libraries Unlimited
A Division of Greenwood Publishing Group, Inc.
Greenwood Village, Colorado

We wish to dedicate this book to all the teachers and students at Bixby High School who continue to encourage and support us. Your comments and compliments each time we change the displays keep our creative juices flowing.

Karen Hawthorne and Jane E. Gibson

Teacher Ideas Press
Libraries Unlimited
A Division of Greenwood Publishing Group, Inc.
7730 East Belleview Avenue, Suite A200
Greenwood Village, CO 80111
1-800-225-5800
www.lu.com

Library of Congress Cataloging-in-Publication Data for Volume 1

Hawthorne, Karen.
    Bulletin boards and 3-D showcases that capture them with pizzazz /
Karen Hawthorne and Jane E. Gibson ; illustrated by Jane E. Gibson.
    ix, 145 p. 22x28 cm.
    Includes index.
    ISBN 1-56308-695-6 (softbound)
    1. Bulletin boards.   I. Gibson, Jane E.   II. Title.
LB1043.58.H38   1999
373. 133'56--dc21
                                                            99-11163
                                                            CIP

Bulletin Boards and 3-D Showcases That Capture Them with Pizzazz, Volume 2
ISBN 1-56308-916-5

Contents

Chapter 2—Putting It Together (*Cont.*)

Chapter 3—Finished Products: Bulletin Boards and Showcases

Chapter 4—Lists, Forms, Sources, Suggestions, and Helps

Introduction

The main objective of bulletin boards and showcase displays should be to capture the attention of students. This is especially a challenge in secondary schools. This challenge is often met by using a multidimensional approach in the presentation. The ideas in this book are designed to attract students in junior and senior high school but can easily be adapted to any grade, subject, and budget.

Bulletin boards are the keys to student input, conversation, excitement, and motivation about reading. An eye-catching, thought-provoking bulletin board may be the beginning of a student becoming a lifelong reader and user of the library. This is especially true of the secondary students who sometimes picture themselves as too "cool" to show enthusiasm about reading.

The bulletin boards featured in this book have been the favorites of students in grades 7–12. Adding a real object (rake, shoes, stuffed animal) seems to attract much more comment and positive responses than the plain, flat displays that are so often used. These bulletin boards speak to the students, and the students respond by saying, "I like that board!"; "Where's that book?"; or even just, "Cool idea."

It is the intention of the authors to facilitate the media specialist's and teacher's jobs when they ponder, "What am I going to put on the bulletin board or showcase this month?"

All bulletin boards and showcases featured in this book have been created by the authors. With a few exceptions, the designs for the bulletin boards and showcases are presented on two facing pages in this book, with bulletin boards on the left and showcases on the right. This format, using facing pages, provides different ideas for using the same theme either as a flat display or as a three-dimensional display. Any resemblance to any design or pictures from any other source is purely coincidental.

In this second volume, we are including the first, second, and fourth chapters of our first book, *Bulletin Boards and 3-D Showcases That Capture Them with Pizzazz,* because without them, the instructions for the 98 new bulletin boards and showcases included here would make no sense to you. Future sequels to these two books will include the same general information found in these instructional chapters. New bulletin boards cannot stand alone and be created unless the definitions and suggestions found in the previous book are included.

Even if you have read the other book, you might want to skim these three chapters again because we constantly update and refine these instructions and helps.

 On the following two pages are photographs of some of the exciting bulletin boards and showcases that we have created. Let them spark your own imagination!

Chapter 1

Getting Started

Bulletin boards come in all shapes and sizes. The most common one, of course, is the typical rectangle shape. However, bulletin boards are not limited to traditional shapes. Bulletin boards may be created using hallways, ceilings, walls, floors, alcoves, doors, windows, corners, and even staircases. A complete wall can become a giant bulletin board that excites and captures the mind of the student or patron. There really are no boundaries for bulletin boards or one's imagination. These display areas may go from ceiling to floor or off each side of the board. Never, ever, let the lack of a bulletin board attached to the wall prevent the creation of exciting and thought-provoking displays. There is no excuse for no bulletin boards. Be creative!

Bulletin boards and showcases are not a luxury. They are necessities. It is a proven fact that students are motivated by visual displays. Students do not always comment about the showcases and boards, but when they do comment they prove the belief that a showcase or bulletin board is worth a hundred words. Seniors have commented about showcases and bulletin boards used in their seventh-grade year when they check out of the library upon graduation. Experts report that students learn 10 percent by listening and 80 percent by viewing. Students also remember 20 percent of what they hear and 50 percent of what they see and hear. These statistics and comments reinforce the crucial need for bulletin boards and displays. They also explain why students do notice and remember these eye-catching efforts.

This chapter includes hints, suggestions, and guidelines that may be followed. These ideas are merely possibilities to improve the showcases, displays, and bulletin boards found in the library and classrooms. However, the bulletin boards featured in this book do not always follow these suggestions. Experiment with these ideas and decide which ones work best for the situations and localities being considered.

PRINCIPLES OF DESIGN

Balance, movement, unity, and simplicity are the four basic principles of design. *Balance* is an important principle to follow. Balance of the bulletin board or project is achieved by the positioning of the elements that have been selected. There are two basic types of balance: formal and informal.

Formal balance uses a symmetrical design and conveys parallel messages. The formal design is divided equally. The props and images project identical reflections if the board is cut in half. These components are usually centered on the board or in the showcase. Most of the boards and showcases in this book employ informal design; however, a striking, simplistic message may be conveyed using a formally designed board.

Informal balance utilizes a more flexible design. Suggestions to remember in informal balance are:

1. Two or more small shapes balance a larger one.

2. A small shape placed low balances a larger one placed high.

3. A brightly colored small shape balances a dull, large shape.

4. A small, interesting, or unusual shape balances a large, ordinary one.

Movement is another design principle, and it should flow toward the center of interest. The logical eye path of the observer should be considered when planning the bulletin board's movement. In the Western world, eye movement is trained to move from left to right and from top to bottom. The eye also is trained to move in a circular motion clockwise. When planning the design, mentally divide the bulletin board into four equal quadrants. The typical eye path starts in the upper left quadrant and retains 41 percent of the initial fixation to the left and above center. Then the eye movement tracks 20 percent into the right upper quadrant and moves downward to the right lower quadrant, where it views only 14 percent. It then continues clockwise into the lower left quadrant, where 25 percent is viewed. The observer's eye initially sees the upper left corner and focuses on the center of interest. The bulletin board artist controls this desired eye movement by using various techniques. String, yarn, ribbon, and other media may be tacked or pinned to the board in a manner that leads the eye to see the whole board arrangement. A good arrangement displays the visual elements in a pattern that captivates the viewer's attention and directs it toward the important details. An imbalance of the board that results in a disproportionate weight distribution of items tends to be psychologically disturbing. Many times, it is very obvious to the trained eye that the board is not balanced. Often this imbalance can be used to an advantage by catching the passing student's fancy. Follow your instincts.

Unity, the third principle of design, is achieved with a sense of cohesion that is reached by the use of space. Unity occurs when the board "clicks" or becomes complete. This completeness may be reached by providing blank space around the visuals and avoiding blank spaces within the visuals that divide it into separate compositions. The usual rule of thumb is less is best. Leave enough space to make the elements grab the viewer's attention.

Simplicity is an important design principle. Limit the number of topics in a visual. Only present one idea at a time. The most common theme of the boards in this book is READ. Many times that four-letter word is the only slogan. It is so simple, but it gets to the heart and purpose of the library. The key is to display something unique that will inspire the student to READ books about the theme of the board or to research that theme.

TOOLS OF DESIGN

There are seven tools of design: space, shape, texture, size, line, arrangement, and color. These tools are all valuable, and an outstanding board is not achieved unless they are implemented.

Space as defined in this section deals with blank space. Space sets objects apart and influences the value, importance, and stability of the visual. The individual elements are emphasized through the use of blank space. Practice with this tool until the comfort zone is reached. Add items, then stand back, take some off and add more to it. Repeat this procedure until the results are pleasing. Trust your intuition.

Shape employs the use of two- and three-dimensional objects. Collect and use a kaleidoscope of shapes and materials, such as corrugated cardboard, Styrofoam, various fabrics, metallic papers such as aluminum foil, shadow boxes, models, and sculptures. Squares, circles, triangles, oblongs, and rectangles add interesting designs to the board and ignite the viewer's interest and imagination. Shape keeps the board from becoming boring or routine.

Texture is an important tool of design. Shoes, feathers, fur, crayons, yarns, mirrors, silk and plastic flowers, gloves, Styrofoam balls, strings, ropes, models, baseball bats, toys, dolls, golf clubs, racquets, and a myriad other objects should be used to attract the student's or patron's interest. These items give the boards texture, and many, of course, get touched and patted. Students love to see real items on the boards and in the showcases. The use of old toys that were once old friends of the students brings back nostalgic memories that halt traffic by the boards. These recycled toys and objects send the students' minds scurrying down memory lane and reinforce the love of reading.

Size is another significant tool of design. Use different sizes of visuals to draw attention to the board. Balance the size of the visual with the lettering. A general rule is to make the lettering 1/25 the height of the visual. However, many times, the slogan or caption is what is being emphasized and the visual is smaller. Experiment with size to achieve the effect that attracts the most attention and best conveys the desired theme.

Line is used in design to direct the attention of the viewer. It is also used to accent the slogan or visual by highlighting it. Examples of line usage would be an arrow as a pointer, a string design pulling the eye toward the desired object of attention, or a simple border drawing attention to one segment of the board.

Arrangement is one of the most versatile tools of design. The placement of visuals to attract attention and to focus on the topic is very important. The arrangement directs the attention to key details. Pin the visuals one way; step back and view the overall effect. Then pin the visuals another way and inspect that arrangement. Many times the arrangement that feels right is the one that should be used. Never forget to experiment with different and unique arrangements.

Color is the most powerful tool of design. Color creates the mood of the board. Excitement is created when red, yellow, or orange is used. A serene mood is created by the use of gray, green, or blue as the dominant color. A mood of peace and contentment is imparted by using blue. Moods of power and vitality are evoked when red is used. To stress strength, reliability, and honesty, use green or red. A mood of security and self-esteem is created when green and blue are used together. There are old rules concerning the use of color, but in today's colorful world, anything goes. However, psychologists still agree that colors do emit certain vibes. Generally accepted interpretations are:

Pinks signify femininity.

Blues signify masculinity.

Browns denote earth tones.

Browns, blacks, whites, and grays are neutral.

Gold is commonly used to highlight dark colors.

Silver is commonly used to highlight light and pastel colors.

Cool colors are blue, green, and violet.

Hot colors are the reds and oranges, and they also signify fire.

Yellow is a warm, bright, happy color and also signifies caution.

Red signifies stop.

Green signifies go.

Blue signifies truth.

Purple signifies royalty.

White signifies purity.

Colors that complement each other are blue/orange; yellow/violet; and red/green. Split complements are red/yellow green/blue green; yellow/red violet/blue violet; and blue/yellow orange/red orange. Three-color schemes that are visually appealing are orange/green/violet and red/yellow/blue.

Analogous colors are three colors side by side on the color wheel. They add attractiveness to the bulletin board and displays. These analogous groups are yellow green/green/blue green; violet/blue violet/red violet; yellow/yellow green/green; blue/blue green/blue violet; blue/blue violet/violet; red/red violet/red orange; orange/red orange/yellow orange; and yellow/yellow orange/yellow green. Use these groups to blend and impart soothing effects on the viewer.

The use of color influences the way the viewer sees the board. The board appears to recede from the observer when cool colors are used. When warm colors are used the board appears to approach the observer. Important cues and slogans in the visual should be highlighted in red and orange to enable the message to leap toward the viewer.

Contrasting colors are used to emphasize points, create mood, provide visual interest, and improve legibility. Monochromatic boards that use only black, white, and grays are quite striking if emphasized with a touch of bright color such as red and blue or blue and yellow. Use contrasting colors for letters and backgrounds to make the board more legible. Green on white; black on yellow; black on white; red on yellow; red on white; and white on black are contrasting colors that increase readability and visibility.

A collection of differently colored backgrounds is essential for the beginning librarian or teacher. Cut the exact size background for your boards and laminate it for repeated use. Basic colors and suggested uses are:

Black—Halloween, Science Fiction, Night Scenes, Space

Brown—Fall, Back to School, Fall Sports

Red—Winter Holidays, St. Valentine's Day, School Colors

Orange—Halloween, Spring, Fall

Yellow—Spring, Summer

Blue—Outdoor Sky, Snow Scenes, Winter, Spring Sky

Green—Spring, St. Patrick's Day, Christmas

White—Snow, Winter

The top or bottom half of any background can be covered with generic meadows, falling leaves, snow banks, and innumerable ground or sky covers. Be creative with color. Use of the color wheel is a definite asset if contrasts and complements are desired. (See figure below.)

Color Wheel

The positive applications of color are many. Color enhances and enriches any bulletin board. Mood influences, emotional responses, and movement indication is achieved by the use and selection of color. Depicting actual colors of the images chosen heightens their realism. Color use points out the similarities and differences of these images. The important information or theme of the board is highlighted by the use of color.

The next step in bulletin board construction is applying the guidelines and suggestions that have been discussed. Remember the basic bulletin board tips that are recommended to incorporate every time:

1. Plan arrangement carefully. Items should be balanced attractively. Slogans should be catchy and grab the viewer's attention.

2. Pin the arrangement before final fastening or stapling. It is easier to rearrange.

3. Change bulletin boards at least once a month; more often is even better.

4. Add real items to add texture, to prevent boredom, and to capture the students' attention.

5. Keep it simple. Less is better. Too much can take away from the desired overall effect.

6. Eye appeal is important. Color is an important factor in catching attention. Black and white can be very dramatic. Use of analogous color schemes on the color wheel can be very eye appealing; however, students today use wild colors together.

7. Be current on student interests. Use your observations of their dress, reading interests, movies, and what they are currently studying. They like to know that the teacher or librarian cares enough to notice. Featuring the summer's blockbuster movie (usually a book) in a back-to-school board or showcase lets the students know that the library is up to date on current trends.

BACKGROUND

Backgrounds are very influential on the overall effect. They "ground" the display and set the basic mood being conveyed. Materials to be used for backgrounds may be as varied as one's imagination. Typical backgrounds are usually constructed from paper, plastic garbage bags, vinyl, and fabric. Remember the aspects of color and texture choices when choosing the background.

Paper of all descriptions may be used. Kraft paper, butcher paper, art paper, construction paper, brown paper sacks, wrapping paper (one of the best choices because of the unlimited scenes and styles), aluminum foil, wallpaper, newspapers, and even sandpaper may be used. The first time that new paper is used for a background, take time to measure the bulletin board and cut the paper to size. This extra time and effort will pay off in future time saved as the background is used again and again. Laminate the backgrounds, if possible, so that they may be reused for years. Do not let the width of the laminator limit making these backgrounds reusable. Just fold the paper in half, cut along the fold, laminate it, then reassemble it on the display. Watch for marked-down wrapping paper or wallpaper patterns that may be useful for backgrounds. Fish, rain forests, stars, and a multitude of themes for backgrounds are available for thrifty prices for the perpetual bulletin board shopper. Many cities have specialty shopping outlets where discontinued patterns are sold daily for at least 50 percent off. Capitalize on the savings found at these outlets.

The use of fabric is unlimited for backgrounds and brings even more unique textures to the board. Bandanna prints; flags; red, white, and blue prints; red and green burlap; velvets; silks; corduroy; and many other fabric scraps found at home or in stores are easily stapled to the bulletin boards for interesting backgrounds and extra texture. One of the most versatile fabric backgrounds used in the showcases in this book is a pastel upholstery piece that has been used to portray gorgeous sunrises and sunsets for beach scenes and Australian and Hawaiian features. Its flexibility has been worth the sale price paid for it 10 years ago. It is used at least once a year. Patterned backgrounds are not drawn into the illustrations of this book because it would make the display too "busy" for the props to be seen on paper.

BORDERS

Borders are an added attraction to showcases and bulletin boards. One must decide whether a border is necessary. If a jungle or outdoor scene is being constructed, then a border might not add anything to it and could in fact detract from its realism. Many of the boards featured in this book were used without a border. If the background material has been cut precisely, then a border may not be necessary. Many times a border is used to cover staples, pins, or raggedy corners. Other objects such as leaves, stars, miniature books, or flowers may be strategically placed to cover staples. Often a border makes the board perfect. The fake-fur Scottie dog bulletin board featured in the first book is an example of the border offering the perfect finishing touch. Finding a border with black-and-white Scotties with bows completed the unique statement this board makes. Borders come from numerous sources. They may be purchased from local teacher supply stores, mail orders, or cut out if student aides or extra time are available. Purchased borders include patterns and solids. Many of the patterned borders look like photographs and add realistic graphics to the board. Solid borders can be quite striking depending upon color choices. Often a border suggests an idea for an entire layout.

Nontraditional borders are created by various applications. Using a leafy vine draped across the top of the board evokes a forest or garden scene. Cotton batting turns the bottom border into a field of snow. Green burlap creates the illusion of grass. Be creative and imaginative with the unlimited possibilities that are available for borders.

Die-cut patterns (such as a leaf, snowflake, or jack-o'-lantern) may be taped together in the exact measurements of the board and then laminated for reuse. These borders create a striking board, especially if that same die-cut pattern is enlarged on the opaque or overhead projector. The enlarged pattern then becomes the center of a completely coordinated board. The result is one of simplicity and often turns into one of the most striking and successful boards created.

LETTERS

Letters are one of the most essential elements of a board or showcase. They can be time-consuming and tedious, but hopefully, the following tips will simplify this chore. Heavy precut letters in a variety of colors and patterns are available for purchase from teacher supply stores or catalogs. These are relatively inexpensive. Begin a basic supply of letters by starting with large and small letters in black, white, and red. Then add other colors and patterns when the budget permits. Many of these packets are coordinated with a matching border. The problem that many librarians and teachers run into with patterned letters is that they are not as versatile as the solids, or often the patterns clash with other backgrounds. These patterned letters work best on a solid background. Use good judgment when making these purchases. A new librarian or teacher just starting out in a career would be wise to purchase these basic colors and laminate them, if possible, to protect this investment.

Purchased pin back letters of one-inch, one-and-one-half-inch, two-inch, two-and-one-half-inch, and three-inch sizes are available in black, white, and red. Begin purchases with the tall white size and add the others as budgets allow. These letters are available from library supply catalogs and local teacher supply stores. One set purchased 30 years ago is still going strong. Its purchase has been well worth the initial investment, even on a beginning teacher's salary or a slim school budget. The time and effort that has been saved by using these letters cannot be stressed enough.

A letter-cutting machine, if available, is a blessing. Use it to cut out letters from construction paper, wrapping paper, card stock, and almost any type of paper that is not too thick. Laminate the paper before cutting for permanence and efficient time management. The time that this machine saves for teachers and librarians is miraculous.

Computer-generated letters give the flexibility of being able to choose unique and numerous fonts and styles (bold, outline, shadow) that complement the theme. Outline is a good choice since it can be colored to match the board design. Type the title as large as possible, then print it. Enlarge it with a copier or opaque projector, depending upon the size desired. Color and laminate it for permanence. This type of lettering can be the most time-consuming, but if the budget or school setting does not have the other options available, this method is superior to freehanding letters or tracing around stencils and cutting them out by hand. The use of colored paper when enlarging slogans and themes also adds dramatic color to the board. The introduction of the computer into print shops and art departments has improved life for the teacher and librarian.

LEAVES AND FLOWERS

Leaves and flowers add new dimensions and textures to the bulletin boards and showcases featured in this book. A good source of artificial leaves and flowers is garage sales. Buy those sad, dusty flower arrangements and fake plants, then dismantle them. Swish silk flowers around in a sink full of warm, sudsy water. Gently shake and hang them upside down to dry, and they are rejuvenated and ready to enhance the boards and showcases. Plastic flowers are also easily washed and dried.

Leaves, especially in autumn colors, may be purchased in the hobby section of large discount stores at a very low cost. Plan ahead for next year and buy them in the postseason markdown sales. It is cost-effective to purchase a leafy "vine," which can be used in a multitude of ways. The vine may become a hanging vine for stuffed animals to hang out on in the showcase or it can be wrapped around the rope of a swing on the bulletin board. These leaves and flowers are added attractions and bring the board or showcase to life. They are especially helpful in plugging holes, covering staples, or balancing the overall effect. There are hundreds of ways that vines and garlands add texture and dimension to these creations. The letter-cutting machine is another resource for leaves and flowers. Many schools have dies for leaves, flowers, and shapes other than letters.

OPAQUE PROJECTOR/OVERHEAD PROJECTOR/ DOCUMENT PROJECTOR

The opaque projector is a valuable tool to help the bulletin board artist. Use the opaque projector to save money and create hard-to-find items. Its use cannot be emphasized enough. Anything that can be found in a picture can be turned into a reproduction for the displays. Items made on the opaque projector are usually flat, so this technique is extremely helpful in creating backgrounds. The opaque projector is also used on fabrics such as fake fur, vinyl, or prints to create creatures and friends for the showcase or board. These items may be produced by implementing the following steps: Use masking tape to fasten a background of poster board, fabric, or other materials to a wall, or staple it directly onto the board. Project the desired picture or design onto the background material, then trace the shape right onto the background. Cut out and laminate. Experiment with different techniques. The overhead projector works in the same manner, but the image must first be transformed into a transparency. Enlarge an image, such as the school emblem or a design desired for use on a piece of poster board, then color it and cut it out. Adding a scrap piece of wood or Styrofoam by gluing it to the back of the image results in a multidimensional board instead of a flat one. Students always notice the school mascots, and this instills school pride; they are especially observant if the mascot is reading.

The photo document camera has simplified the reproduction of props. The clarity of the object is much better and it's easier to reproduce. The procedure for enlarging graphics is basically the same as for the opaque projector.

MISCELLANEOUS PROPS

Many of these boards are purely motivational. Students really notice giant candy canes, bugs, real shoes, or kites in the media center. Try to make books and reading fun as well as exciting. Multiple copies of booklists can be printed, allowing students and faculty to take one for their personal use. A "take one" box for these lists can be made by cutting an empty cereal box in half, then covering it with a neutral contact paper. This can be used repeatedly.

There are numerous miscellaneous props that enhance bulletin boards and showcases. Many items on the basic supplies list are already available at the school library or at home. Garage sales, postholiday sales, and spring cleaning yield exciting props, ideas, and decorations. Twigs and branches from the yard, unclaimed scarves and mittens from the lost-and-found, colorful pictures from donated magazines, and children's old toys spark ideas for creative, eye-catching bulletin boards. The recycling of kids' toys or toys from garage sales cannot be emphasized enough. These toys capture many of the most reluctant readers; invariably, they are overheard saying, "I had one of those, but my mom threw it out." The memories of the fun experienced with these toys transfers to the fun of the play on words that might inspire them to read a book from the featured genre or theme. One major rule that cannot be stressed enough is always keep your eyes and mind open to the unlimited ideas from which bulletin boards can be created.

To create "bubbles" for underwater scenes, carefully cut around individual large and small air cells in bubble wrap used for packing. The wrap comes in a variety of colors.

If the props suggested in this book cannot be located, use something else. These illustrations and instructions are only suggestions to inspire ideas unique to each classroom or library setting.

Many of the drawn or constructed paper props can be reused. Save the fireplace, once made, and use it in the coming years. Store it in a drawer in a map case. Likewise, laminate the "grass" strips and many of the props made from patterns for future use.

STORAGE

After the librarian or teacher starts collecting treasures and props for the bulletin board, a big problem arises: How are these fabulous discoveries and creations going to be kept for future use? Empty computer and duplicating paper boxes are excellent storage compartments for bulletin board supplies. They are a convenient size for easy handling and storage in almost any facility. Because some supplies and props are used in many different displays, trying to keep a box for each board theme is not the most efficient method. Experience has proven that it is better to store like components together in labeled boxes; for example, all leaves in one box, letters in another, background fabrics in yet another. The generic items such as leaves, seashells, trees, and cotton batting found on the supply list should be labeled and stacked alphabetically to facilitate locating and speedily changing the boards monthly.

The boxes can be neatly stacked upon each other, stored on shelves or under worktables. Label them plainly on both ends with a permanent marker. If there is too much writing on the ends of the boxes, paint over it with a craft paint or tape a clean piece of paper onto the ends of the box (the painting option would be more permanent). Then label the boxes. Drawers in a map case are perfect for storing posters, slogans, and large pictures. There are various oversized storage cartons available for purchase. Look through supply catalogs for other ideas on storage, but a map case works best of all. A file cabinet can also be used to store letters and slogans. Use the length of the drawers to make lateral files by cutting cardboard in the appropriate lengths to divide the drawers into sections. These pieces of cardboard can be labeled with the slogans and makes finding them much easier. Slogans and words that have been laminated in strips may be stored in this manner.

Background papers may be rolled loosely, held with a rubber band, and stored in large trash cans. A smaller can may be used for shorter rolls. The rolls may be labeled by small writing on the reverse side of a corner of the paper or by inserting a label under the rubber band holding the rolls.

Chapter 2

Putting It Together

Developing the display is the next step in becoming a master of bulletin board and showcase creations. Generally, there are months and holidays for which ideas are easily generated. Other times, it is very difficult even to begin thinking about what to do that month. Historically, back-to-school time seems to be a difficult time to decide what to feature. Students have been having a good time working or doing summertime activities, and they are not necessarily thinking about getting back to reading and researching. This lack of interest is normal and challenges the bulletin board artist to entice them back into the library. On the one hand, January always seems to be another time that is difficult to decide what to create; these problem months require even more effort to create unusual and innovative displays. On the other hand, fall seems to be an easy season for generating slogans for theme boards and showcases. Scarecrows, autumn leaves, ornamental corn, and hay bales are quickly assembled to carry out these seasonal ideas. Back up the autumn showcase or bookcase display with fall bulletin boards and displays throughout the area. Sports themes work well during their respective seasons; posters of sports figures can be used to promote almost any subject.

Another consideration in developing holiday displays is local community preferences and its views on the subject of holiday observances in the schools. Most public schools allow holiday displays involving Halloween, Thanksgiving, and some variation of the December holidays: Hanukkah, Christmas, and other multicultural celebrations. If local opinion prefers, October can be represented with a football, softball, or soccer theme instead of Halloween. Santa Claus is generally accepted for the Yule season. In private schools, or where allowed, religious holidays offer opportunities to display wonderful collections of crèches, menorahs, and dreidels borrowed from faculty and staff. Thanksgiving can be depicted historically (pilgrims), mathematically (how many quarter-pound servings from a 21-pound turkey?), or to emphasize reading ("Give Thanks for Books"). St. Valentine's Day does not have to be limited to heart cutouts. A display of "Heartbreakers and Tearjerkers" or the familiar "Books We All Love" can highlight romance novels or classic favorites. Local opinion and preferences often suggest appropriate ways to handle the development of displays.

The librarian or teacher should develop a bulletin board or showcase by implementing the following guidelines:

1. Decide upon an objective.

2. Generate a theme.

3. Incorporate the theme into a slogan.

4. Work out a rough layout.

5. Gather the materials.

6. Put up the display.

OBJECTIVE

Deciding upon the objective is sometimes the hardest step in getting started. The most often asked question after a showcase or board is put up is, "Where do you get your ideas?" or "Do you have a book of ideas?" or "How do you come up with these great ideas?" Almost every faculty member says, "You ought to write a book to help us out!" They seem to have no trouble imagining these ideas transformed into their subject content.

Basically, ideas are collected from everywhere if teachers and librarians train themselves to look for opportunities to turn anything into a way to promote reading, books, and the various curriculum areas. The bulletin board and showcase artist can usually transform any idea or advertising campaign into an appealing board or showcase. The most common inspirations for the boards and showcases in this book are generated from shopping; television ads and programs; newspaper ads and stories; advertisements; garage sales; flea markets; current trends and fads (often the products from this category are not used over and over because these trends and fads do not last long); catalogs; collections (personal ones of staff and students); home; unlikely places; the Internet; and brainstorming. Ideas are triggered from a multitude of sources; do not be limited by the usual concepts. For example, a background of hearts was combined with a student's collection of stuffed toy monkeys and gorillas reading favorite books in the showcase. Adding Spanish moss, artificial leaf garlands, plastic ferns, and indoor-outdoor carpeting was all that was needed to create a jungle setting for an unorthodox variation of the Valentine slogan "Read to Your Sweetheart." The mind must be kept open to the possibility of ideas cropping up anywhere.

SHOPPING

Go shopping. "Shop 'til you drop" and never run out of ideas. Go to the hobby shops, toy stores, craft stores, any store, and OBSERVE. Stroll down those sale aisles. Search for something that is unique. Take those advertising banners and aisle teasers; twist them and bend the slogans into something about reading or a theme for the teacher's subject area. Be open to ideas while shopping. End-of-season sales are a good source for wallpaper and wrapping paper that can be used for backgrounds. Holiday decorations and inexpensive toys such as plastic rakes, tools, inflatable skeletons, and more are often found at the end-of-season sales. Start collecting anything that suggests a theme, such as the toy rake ("Rake in a Good Book"); toy shovel ("Dig into Reading—or Math, English, Science"); toy bugs ("Buggy About Books"); and toy grasshoppers ("Hop into Reading"). These are just a few ideas and suggestions of items that can be found while shopping and then used to create an eye-catching board. A postseason sale on costumes for dolls inspired a *Wizard of Oz* showcase; once the costumes were bought, very few other items had to be purchased. The pastel background and green burlap in this showcase were from the basic supplies list. An inexpensive piece of yellow vinyl was bought to make the yellow brick road. It was cut to show perspective, and bricks were drawn on using a Sharpie pen. One small bouquet of silk poppies was disassembled to make a field of poppies by sticking the individual flowers into the burlap. The "Emerald City" was created inexpensively from rolled tubes of newspaper that were sprayed with green paint. These tubes were then sprinkled with glitter and glued together. Cotton batting from the basic supplies list was pulled apart to create a "mist" around the city. This showcase was quite popular and it sprang into being with finds of doll costumes on sale. Shopping generates hundreds of ideas and costs nothing if ideas are all that are gained. Often, the ideas come and then useful items lying around the house or school are recruited to implement them. Yes, shopping could be expensive if one is a compulsive shopper, but many shopping trips have inspired themes that utilized existing props in the library, classrooms, or home.

TELEVISION

Of course, there is no better source of ideas for capitalizing on the love of reading than the television. Popular television shows create an interest that, if teachers and librarians are able to duplicate it, can attract students and keep their love of reading going strong. Examples of this technique are numerous: "Tool Time" easily becomes "Tool Time Reading" using hammers, screwdrivers, pliers, and other tools for props and highlighting the woodworking and carpentry books from the library. The possibilities are limitless. While channel surfing, pay attention to ads. Commercials such as "Like a Rock" for Chevy trucks easily jogs the mind into creating the slogan "Rocky Reading," which features books on rocks and geology, or it could easily become "Reading Rocks" featuring the rock-music books. Cultivate the ability to capitalize on the opportunity that television offers for finding unique and appealing ideas when the mind is trained to look for them.

NEWSPAPERS

Newspapers generate a multitude of ideas for boards and showcases. Play a mental game by selecting any advertisement and transforming it into an advertisement for reading or subject content. "Moonlight Madness" sales are featured throughout the year in the newspaper. This theme logically leads into use in October with a huge, orange harvest moon, the generic showcase tree with an owl or skeleton sitting in it, and the transformed slogan "Moonlight Reading Madness," featuring mysteries or horror books. Play this mental game to train the brain, often, to find new and unique ideas that the students have not seen in every classroom or library. Notice the want ads and sports sections of the newspapers. Often catchy phrases and some of the best descriptive writing is found in the sports page: "Spartans Roll Over Cowboys" could easily inspire a perceptive librarian into featuring new books and naming the board "Roll into the Library for a New Book."

ADVERTISEMENTS

Advertisements in newspapers, stores, magazines, the Internet, road signs, billboards, airports, shopping malls, television, and anywhere inspire slogans. Be observant to see if these ads can be scrambled, realigned, or redesigned to become a bulletin board or showcase message. Retail stores receive coordinated sales and ad campaigns at least four times a year during each of the four seasons. Repeat and reword these slogans to emphasize reading and other curriculum needs. Target reading, just like the advertising pros target their markets, to inspire students to become lifetime readers.

GARAGE SALES

Garage sales are an excellent source for ideas. Artificial plants, flower arrangements, toys, and props can be disassembled and used repeatedly in a variety of combinations. One never knows what great inexpensive discovery is lurking at a garage sale. A miniature stove ("Hot Reading"), cowboy boots ("Boot-Scootin' Books"), a sewing machine ("Books Are 'Sew' Good"), toy animals, and endless other cast-off treasures can be utilized when purchased with a theme in mind. Buy inexpensive racquets, golf clubs, and ball bats for a board and showcase titled "Swing into Spring Reading." Make a resolution to explore garage sales when looking for props or ideas.

CURRENT TRENDS AND FADS

Current trends are indispensable sources for ideas. Slogans from the summer's hottest movie often make great back-to-school boards. A *Terminator* movie poster had the slogan "I'm Back!" "I'm" was changed to "We're Back!" then "To Reading" was added. Posters from movies make simple and easy bulletin boards to construct, and the students are glad to see something or someone they like inviting them to enjoy books and reading. Storage drawers and cabinets are filled with the same old back-to-school red apples, same old yellow buses, pencils, rulers, and schoolhouses. None of them inspires reading. Many of these cardboard items have been seen so many times in each of the students' classes since kindergarten that they have become invisible. Students just do not see them or pay any attention to them by the time they get to the secondary school level. Today's students need something they like to grab their attention. Rock stars, sports stars, Internet themes, and body piercing may be in and out, but there are always things and people that inspire students. Try to focus on these likes and use them in a way that is positive for reading or subject area content. Be aware of what the current trends are and capitalize on their popularity. Displays on scary books are always a big attraction. *Star Wars* is a good example of a fad that often becomes a classic: *Star Wars* gets a lot of attention, however and whenever it is chosen to be used. Students are surprised to find out that classics are not all "thick, boring books." A striking board or showcase can highlight *Dracula*, *A Connecticut Yankee in King Arthur's Court*, *Of Mice and Men*, and *The Secret Garden*, which are all favorite classics that are in constant circulation. These classics are in great demand, especially after a new movie version has been released. Do not miss the opportunity to capitalize on the current movie's popularity.

CATALOGS

Every library and teacher gets hundreds of catalogs and junk mail. Turn this junk into sources of innovative boards and showcases. Budgets often restrict how many kits and items can be purchased. Order what money allows and create the rest. Many miniature books that creatures and characters read on the boards and in the showcases featured in this book are cut out from vendor catalogs. These colorful reproductions are easily glued onto card stock and folded into a book. Students laugh at some of the titles the props are reading. A duck showcase, for example, featured the mother duck reading Art Linkletter's book, *Kids Say the Darndest Things*, while the little ducks following her were reading *High Flying*, *The Stealth Fighter Pilot*, and *Be an Olympic Swimmer*. Students and faculty notice this sense of humor and feel more welcomed in the library. They often stop in just to remark about the humorous titles. Catalogs are a very valuable source of ideas and items for the boards and showcases.

COLLECTIONS

Almost everybody collects something; some people collect everything. Search those people out when hard-to-find objects are needed. It is amazing what can be found if a note is placed in the school paper or bulletin. Students and faculty love to see their collections being used. Many times a showcase has inspired a faculty member or student to remark, "I have a collection of eagles, or author dolls, or owls, or cows if you ever want to use them." One faculty member has offered an 18-inch Emily Dickinson doll to use. It has not been borrowed yet, but it is on the planning sheet of possibilities.

INTERNET

One source of ideas being explored more and more is the Internet. This source may become the best asset because most of the suggested resources already mentioned are now available on the Internet (even shopping). Just type in a subject, think, brainstorm, and imagine. Thousands of sources will come up to help decide the theme or slogan. It takes time, but it is a gold mine of ideas. Some suggested sites are clipart.com (free clip art, fonts, and graphics); Barrysclipart.com; iconbazaar.com; and CoolText.com. These addresses are current as of publication date.

BRAINSTORM

Brainstorm with fellow workers, family, student aides, and anyone who will listen. Write down slogans and ideas as they occur, no matter how far-fetched or unlikely they sound. Do not evaluate these ideas until they stop materializing. Then go back and discuss them for possible use. Keep a file by subject or theme. A simple recipe box with index cards is a convenient place to store ideas for future reference; reading through the cards can start different trains of thought. Sometimes it is very helpful to "sleep on it." The next day, one of the brainstormed ideas gels and becomes the exact one wanted, or suddenly a way is perceived to make it even more appealing.

UNLIKELY PLACES

Do not forget to expect great ideas to pop up in unlikely places. An "Un-'Bull'-ievable Books" showcase was the result of seeing a fan holding up a sign at a Chicago Bulls game that was being televised. This sighting sparked a showcase featuring a Michael Jordan doll, a miniature basketball hoop, a towel with the Bulls logo, and books about basketball. It got rave reviews by students and faculty. A fabric store selling "Boot-Scootin'" material inspired a "Boot-Scootin' Books" showcase featuring the Western genre. Student aides helped place the boots so that they appeared to be line dancing. Just talking with coworkers often produces dozens of ideas. Choose one that works. Let people know that suggestions for new designs and input are very welcome, and never forget to be thinking about themes and slogans in unlikely places.

HOME

Look around home and school for objects that tie into the selected themes. Small chunks of firewood, stuffed animals, travel souvenirs, fabric scraps, doll furniture, and old clothes are just a few of the items that have been called into service over the years. Those toys and items that are not used now, but are of too much sentimental value to discard, become the best props to use. Dig these items out of the attic and closets and make them useful.

THEME

Once an idea is generated from these different sources, a theme is the next step in developing a bulletin board display. Often the props or items automatically scream out the theme, just as the toy rake, shovel, and miniature stove did. If a theme is not obvious, start brainstorming until a theme is in place; then incorporate this theme into a slogan.

SLOGANS

The slogan should usually be short and to the point. Play word games; many times the best headline or slogan is not the first idea. An example of this game playing would be to decide to feature classic books. Finding a poster of Leonardo DiCaprio from *Romeo and Juliet* was the catalyst for this board; the theme, of course, was classic reading. Brainstorming resulted in these possible slogans: "Read a Classic," "Classic Reads," "Shakespeare Is Classic," and "Leo Recommends These Classics." Many other ideas could be generated for this board, but these are enough to illustrate this technique. "Read a Classic" was the one chosen for the headline. Often the other choices are equally motivating. Try to implement the catchiest and most thought-provoking slogan.

LAYOUT SKETCH

The next step in getting started is to make a rough layout. A small sketch is helpful to visualize the overall effect; implementing the sketch is often trial and error. Next, collect the items for the board or showcase. Sometimes it has taken several years to gather all the items needed to create some of the best showcases, so whenever a unique idea pops up, jot it down and start gathering the materials. Sketch the layout, and as props are procured, check them off the sketch. This technique enables organization that is beneficial and helpful in getting the final product completed.

FINAL PRODUCT

The final step is putting up the display. Remember to experiment with different arrangements by pinning up the items. When the best arrangement is chosen, staple everything to stabilize it. Stay open to new ideas, rearrangements, and wording changes as the display is constructed. The end result is often different from the preliminary sketch. The final arrangement is often the result of trial and error. Keep experimenting until the layout is pleasing and satisfactory.

COSTS

Often colleagues look at the bulletin boards and showcases and comment that they do not have the money to make their boards and showcases look like these. It is not necessary to spend a lot of money to provide exciting and challenging showcases and bulletin boards. Most of the featured items have been inexpensive. If a miniature washer and dryer set is not easily found, use the overhead or opaque projector to make one. Computer paper boxes are easily transformed into a washer or dryer by stapling or hot gluing a top onto the back of the box and then cutting a lid from the top or front. Paint the inside of the lid white. Many times the decision for the type of props used is determined by the librarian's or teacher's availability of money and resources. Many kits are available from library supply catalogs. Many single items are available but are often expensive. Most of the boards and showcases in this book, and often the most popular ones, are created as they are constructed. Don't buy everything listed under props. This could become expensive. Look around and improvise, substitute, or borrow. Change the title to fit your resources. Reuse props from other displays. Set your imagination free.

ON-SITE CONSTRUCTION

On-site construction is often the only way to complete gathering just the right materials. One does not have to be an artist to make most items. Remember to be on the lookout for anything to illustrate good ideas and be open to whatever crops up. When the right item cannot be found, make it! An inflatable skeleton was inflated and then wrapped in strips of muslin to become a needed mummy. A scrap piece of vinyl was painted to create a teepee. If there is no washer or dryer to be found and making one does not happen, substitute a small plastic or straw laundry basket heaped with doll or baby clothes, donated or bought at garage sales. Add a child's toy ironing board and iron, and then scatter clothespins and miniature detergent boxes (found at most laundromats) to complete the wash-day scene. A scarecrow is easily made on-site by using stuffed panty hose to form a body. Two pairs of these stuffed hose may be tied together or sewn together to make legs and arms. Next, dress the scarecrow in old clothes; the head can be sewn from scraps and stuffed or even made from a brown paper sack with the face drawn on with markers. Finish the scarecrow by gluing on yarn or raffia for hair. Another option for the face would be to sew it out of muslin and embroider a face for a more permanent addition to the prop stock. When the scarecrow is not used in the showcase, it makes a perfect addition to a display of fall or horror books when placed at the end of the bookshelves in the library. Tornadoes are easily made from quilt stuffing or batting. These are just a few ideas of needed items that were produced by on-site construction.

PLANNING SHEETS

A planning sheet is convenient, both for a record of displays used and as an ongoing idea planner. Two different planning sheets have been developed to easily show what has been featured. The planning sheet for each month has room for 17 years. It is easy to see when a board was featured. Also included is a yearly planning sheet; brainstorming usually fills the margins with ideas for the year. Boards and showcases are rotated so that the students never see them more than once during their secondary school years. Exceptions are made for certain showcases that students request and ask to be put back up, but generally a board or showcase is never used again until the youngest class that saw it first has graduated. Many of the same props are used over with different slogans and headlines. Sample planning sheets are included in Chapter Four. These planning sheets are very helpful and the librarian or teacher can readily decide if enough time has elapsed between usage of the boards. It is suggested that pencil be used on planning sheets, because many times current events or local programs require rapid changes in these plans.

THEME CATEGORIES

Suggestions to feature for boards and showcases include different genres of literature, local color and interests, contests, weather, travel, hobbies, special events, current events, sports, month-by-month events, and miscellaneous.

LITERARY GENRES

The different genres of literature spark student interest when featured in the showcase or on bulletin boards. These genres may be featured any time of the year, although some definitely complement the different seasons, for example, mysteries and horror for fall and Halloween. Be sure to develop boards and displays for these genres: Science Fiction, Fantasy, Historical Fiction, Romance, Sports, Horror, Mysteries, Westerns, Travel, Biographies, and Classics.

LOCAL COLOR AND INTERESTS

Most communities have festivals and parades that feature local color and themes of local interests. Green Corn Festivals, Pumpkin Festivals, and Herb-and-Plant Festivals are just a few hosted locally in this part of Oklahoma. These local activities are great ways to promote reading and increase public awareness and public relations. The *Phantom of the Opera* board and showcase are great for October, but were also used when *Phantom of the Opera* toured neighboring cities. The Egyptian showcase would be appropriate any time, but especially when the King Tut and other Egyptian exhibits are touring nearby. Be certain to capitalize on these opportunities of local interests.

CONTESTS

Contest boards and showcases are very popular items. Anything that allows participation from the students draws interest. Contests attract students, faculty, and staff and are usually held in conjunction with National Library Week in April. The "How Many . . . ?" contests can be a hit. "Books: The Key to Success" featured books on testing, education, and scholarships. It challenged the participants to guess how many keys were in the showcase. Students were lured into the contest by a blue-and-gold wrapping-paper background accented with big "brass" (plaster) keys. Sitting in the middle of the showcase was the ever-useful pedestal supporting a clear plastic container (used to hold candy in the concession stand) full of old, discarded keys borrowed from the local locksmith. Prizes for the closest guess to the correct number of keys in the container were awarded to a junior high student, a senior high student and a faculty or staff member. Other successful contest promotions include "How Many Books in the Showcase?" and "How Many Cups of Popped Corn in the Bag?"

WEATHER

Weather is always fascinating to students, perhaps because it changes so often, affects lives so much, cannot be controlled, and is rarely predicted. Do not overlook the occasion to use the weather to promote reading excitement. For example: "Winter Brings Good Knights to Read" (using knights and castles); "Warm Up with Reading" (a snowman reading a book); and "Be Cool This Summer . . . Read" (cool cat reading amid a beach scene) are just a few weather examples. "Fan-tastic Books for Summer" is a May bulletin board that has been used more than once with positive results. It encourages summer reading and gives book suggestions. April showers, March winds, and spring fever are all great weather themes to be featured.

TRAVEL

Travel themes are popular and capture student interest in geography and traveling throughout the world. Theme boards and showcases attract the students' attention with the use of catchy puns and eye-grabbing displays. "Book an Adventure" has been a successfully repeated theme, varying the destination. A trip to the Orient incorporates travel posters, fans, dolls, a kimono, and a floral background with a display of books about the Orient and origami. Australia can be highlighted with koalas hanging onto the generic library tree decorated with eucalyptus leaves.

HOBBIES

Hobby themes always trigger comments from students and especially from the young men who sometimes never say anything. Fishing is very popular in the Midwest, and a fishing theme stops traffic outside the library. The fish that hook their attention may be found at the local fabric store. A printed block of material depicting fish is cut out, sewn, and stuffed. Then the resulting stuffed fish are hung from a stringer or posed jumping at a lure. Pictures or cutouts of fish can be substituted for the cloth ones. Stuffed fish are also available for purchase at various retail stores. Fishing poles and a hat complement the fishy wrapping-paper background. A display of books on fishing and science books about fish complete the theme "Get Hooked on Reading." This theme could be used as "Get

Hooked on Math" (English, history, or whatever the subject may be). Use formulas, adjectives, or dates for the lures and transfer the idea to a bulletin board. A dowel rod and string make a fine fishing pole for a board display. Other hobbies such as racing, bird watching, boating, and skiing could easily be featured and will be guaranteed traffic stoppers.

SPECIAL EVENTS

Special events should be featured to include areas that sometimes do not fit into other categories. National months, multicultural events, and the Olympics fit into this area. The Summer and Winter Olympics, the elections, the Gulf War, the War Against Terrorism, Miss America and her platform, or graduation all present themes for display. Incorporate newspaper articles, posters, and items found around the house to effectively highlight these subjects. During the Gulf War and the War Against Terrorism, the daily news releases, along with a laminated map published in the local newspaper, were posted. The title of the board was "Read All About It," and it attracted both adults and students. Multicultural commemorations such as Deaf Awareness Week, Native American History Month, and Women's History Month are good selections for their respective dates. Remember to include National Library Week in April.

SPORTS

When featuring sports and sports teams, consider using their team colors for the background on the boards and showcases. One might use red and black for the Chicago Bulls and blue and gray for the Dallas Cowboys. Posters of current sports stars are always available at local retail shops. Students also stop to take notice of their favorite pro stars reading. Many sports figures have also made the READ posters for the American Library Association (ALA). These stars are very important to the students. Often, the most reluctant readers cannot resist a board or showcase that features their favorite sports star. Make the most of the influence that sports play in the life of the secondary school student. Use this influence to induce those reluctant readers to check out books to read about their favorite sports stars. Such readers will usually return for another book once they are hooked.

KITS

Complete bulletin board kits are available for purchase from several library companies. A list of vendors is provided in the Suggested Resources at the end of Chapter Four. Most of these kits furnish flat items and props. Do not forget that these captions and slogans are usable in new creations, too. The convenience of having a kit ready to slap up on the board is a plus. Experience has shown that these kits do not attract the interest and comments of the students and faculty as much as the three-dimensional ones featured in this book. However, many scheduling conflicts, peak usage times, and life in general have proven the need to have something that can be put up at a moment's notice. These kits are invaluable tools to have on hand for these emergencies. After librarians and teachers have created several of the boards and showcases in this book, they will notice that they have in fact created their own kits with three-dimensional objects. These kits are not available for purchase and are not seen everywhere. Just as it is never a chosen scenario to appear at a social gathering and find several people wearing the same apparel, it is also not appealing to have every classroom and library decorated with the same bulletin board. Be unique.

POSTERS

Posters attract a lot of student attention. Posters of rock stars, cars, pets, and other items of popular interest are also available for purchase. Captions that stress reading can be written or typed and enlarged on the copier or computer. Then these captions can be taped onto or around the posters. Examples of posters used successfully for bulletin boards are many. One successful usage was a poster picturing a dalmation sitting in front of a chalkboard filled over and over with "I will not bark in class." This poster was transformed into a reading awareness poster by adding a balloon caption that stated, "I shoulda been reading!" Strips of paper with names of helpful reading matter such as *The Student Handbook*, *Rules*, and *Emily Post's Book of Etiquette* were placed strategically around the poster. Another successful poster portrayed a shar-pei dog wearing glasses, hair curlers, and an old housedress; the shar-pei was ironing. There was no caption, so the caption "Get a Life . . . Read" was added. This poster caused the students to stop, laugh, and comment about it. It got their attention and, perhaps, planted the idea that a person who reads has a more meaningful life. Another popular poster pictured three shar-pei puppies wearing baby bonnets and standing up in a baby bed with the slogan "Rise and Whine." The slogan "It's Reading Time" was added and transformed these babies into reading promoters. Mickey Mouse wallpaper was chosen for the background and made the puppies look as if they were in a nursery. Posters add a lot of fun. Some posters cannot be resisted because they are so cute. Their use to promote and stress reading and other curriculum areas is very beneficial to the students.

PATTERNS

Colleagues and students constantly ask, "Where did you get that?" If items are not easily found and must be made for the showcase, new problems arise. Where is an easily reproduced pattern of the object to be found? There are many resources. Coloring books are excellent sources because they have dark, clean lines and project well on the wall when using the opaque projector. The simpler the drawing, the easier it is to reproduce. Clip art on CD-ROM, the Internet, and in books also make excellent sources for patterns. Cutouts from old greeting cards, newspapers, magazines, discarded books, coloring books, and workbooks can be used to obtain patterns to use for the bulletin boards and showcases. Using these patterns and the opaque projector to enlarge them on paper, cardboard, fake fur, and other materials results in soft sculptures and items that complete unique displays. Other sources of patterns can be found in picture files, government agencies, and commercial shops. Often, the art and woodworking department will collaborate on artwork and patterns. Be certain to give plenty of advance notice when working with these groups. The illustrations of the bulletin boards and showcases in Chapter Three will make excellent patterns to use on the opaque projector.

DONATIONS

Get the word out that donations of props and items are needed and accepted. After an Egyptian showcase was featured, a perfect reproduction of a Nefertiti bust with an accompanying podium and Plexiglas cover was donated to the school system. The administration left it housed in the library, where it will make a priceless addition to the next Egyptian showcase. In the meantime, Nefertiti reigns over the library and sparks many a study in researching her life and times. Since the publication of our first book, an entire collection of books on Egyptology has been donated to our media center. It is amazing what may find its way to the library when the patrons, public, and staff become aware of its needs.

Now is the time to assemble the bulletin boards, displays, and showcases. But first, a few explanations, descriptions, and helpful hints for following the instructions for the construction of showcases and bulletin boards should be discussed. Dimensions and lengths of props for the displays are purposely left out in most cases because boards and showcases come in all sizes. Always measure material before cutting or buying to be certain that enough has been purchased.

TREE

The tree displayed in many of the showcases is just a tree limb picked up from the yard. Find one that is approximately as tall as the showcase in which it is going to be used. As the seasons change, so does this tree. Green leaves are taped, stapled, or pinned to it to create a summer or springtime tree. Fall leaves are similarly fastened to it to change the season to autumn. Cotton batting is laid on its branches to evoke a snowy day. Animals cling to its branches, sit in it, read in it and under it. Its use is unlimited. Placing the tree in the foreground of the showcase gives extra dimension and texture to the display. Placing the tree in a back corner gives the illusion of extra depth. Move the tree around. Try different placements to vary the showcase appearance and scenery.

SLINGS

The sling is a support used to display books on the showcase walls and bulletin boards. Use of the sling enables using real books instead of book jackets. Book jackets may then be left on the book to protect it. These strips of material, string, ribbon, or laminating film make it possible to display the actual books in attractive arrangements without damaging the volume. Cut a strip about one inch wide from the selected material. From this piece, cut a strip about 5 to 10 inches long, depending upon the size of the book. It is desirable to have approximately two inches extra for each book so that this excess can be stapled to the board. Staple the ends of the strip to the background horizontally or at a slight angle where desired. Either insert the bottom corner of the book behind the strip as far down as possible, or open the book and insert half the pages behind the sling as if it were a bookmark. Larger volumes may need a wider, stronger material. Examples of these two slings can be seen in the displays "Pilgrim Tales" (p. 62) and "Trim the Tree with Holiday Reading" (p. 76).

RUBBER CEMENT

This versatile adhesive turns any lightweight object into a seemingly suspended item simply by applying a dab of it to the object and pressing it against the inside of the glass showcase door, a window, or directly to the laminated background of the bulletin board. Raindrops fall, snowflakes drift, fish swim, stars shine, butterflies flutter, and bugs buzz at eye level right before the student's eyes; the cement is invisible. This technique adds more dimension and flair to the scene. When the display is dismantled, gently pull off the rubber cement and rub any residue off the glass. This technique works best if the item is laminated or made of a nonporous material, such as aluminum foil raindrops or stars. Items may be created by using an opaque projector, computer clip art, a die-cutting machine, or freehand cuttings.

FLOORING

Carpet strips cut to the exact size of the showcase floor give a finishing touch to the scene being created. Artificial turf can set an outdoor theme. Cut a second piece of artificial turf; touch it up with dabs of brown, red, orange, and gold paint; it then becomes an autumn ground cover. White carpet turns the scene into winter. If the base is already wood, take advantage of that for indoor exhibits and use it as a base for a small throw rug or make it into a gym floor. Use those vacation seashells to create a beach scene! Be innovative!

SHOWCASE CEILING

Items may be suspended by hanging them on fishing line, which is taped to the surface if the showcase has a solid ceiling. This technique gives the illusion of birds in flight or snowflakes falling, or it supports an ivy vine twisting itself across the case. If the ceiling has movable tiles or light cover, take advantage of the support strips to hang various props. A length of coat hanger cut to fit between the supports is used as a beam from which different lengths of fishing line with props are tied. By employing two or more of these rods, it becomes possible to suspend everything: snowflakes, leaves, sports racquets, animals, holiday ornaments, and anything else imaginable.

SPECIAL EFFECTS

A cloud background can be created from a package of computer paper printed with a cloud design. The sheets are taped together in strips the width of the bulletin board and also in widths to fit the showcase. Then laminate these strips. Another source for special effects is wrapping paper with similar cloud designs and items such as stars, snowflakes, and lightning, which enhance outdoor theme boards and showcases.

If large rolls of art kraft paper are available at your school, cut pieces in various colors to fit the width of the board and the showcase background. These pieces are then cut in half lengthwise and laminated. The strips are now ready to be cut, freehand, into strips of green grass, blue waves, white drifts of snow, or brown hills.

Small pieces of Styrofoam can be used in order to produce a three-dimensional effect on bulletin boards and showcases. Save Styrofoam scraps for this purpose. Little squares can be glued to the backs of letters, stars, leaves, or miniature book covers to give depth to the display. Larger strips or blocks turn a napkin into a tablecloth on a table or make a character stand out from the board. Foam packing can become "popcorn" when put into small sacks or boxes obtained from a concession stand. Strips of Styrofoam can be purchased or found in packing materials. Using foam board to create props also adds dimension and alleviates the boredom of flat objects. A tip to remember about cutting Styrofoam is to rub the knife on a candle to coat it with wax; it will then be able to slice through the Styrofoam without having to saw.

ELEVATION

Sometimes it is desirable to elevate the showcase displays to achieve the correct eye level and to center props and slogans to add interest or highlight a theme. Use books or boxes as a platform by making level or unequal stacks to the height or heights needed. Cover the stacks with draped material to create the desired effect. Green burlap simulates a grassy hill, white velvet or cotton batting portrays snow drifts, while black trash bags against a black background set an eerie mood.

The individual size of showcases determines the need for elevation. The size of props also determines when to implement elevation and different elevations. When fashion dolls or small collectible items are used, elevation becomes very important.

Chapter 3

Finished Products: Bulletin Boards and Showcases

TITLES:

I Should'a Read The Rulz

Read The Rulz!

Start The Year Right! Read The Rulz

BACKGROUND: Black

BORDERS: Purchased school or classroom theme

LETTERING: White three-inch pin backs

PROPS: Black paper; chalk or white ink pen; strips of wallpaper or colored paper; small doll; pushpins; student handbook for your school; list of classroom rules

INSTRUCTIONS: Fasten the background to the board. Pin the title down the left half of the board. Fasten a strip of paper across the bottom of the right half to make a "wall" beneath a "blackboard." Use strips of paper to frame the rest of the "blackboard" and fasten the border around the entire board. A small blackboard could be used with the doll instead of just the paper. A purchased poster of a child writing on a blackboard or dogs with a blackboard saying, "I will not bark in class" is another option. Pin the doll in front of the "board" on the right side. With the chalk or pen write school rules or "I will not…" type sentences on the "board." Pin a copy of the school rules to the board.

TITLES:

Back 2 The Books

Back 2 School Reading

Back 2 School Books

BACKGROUND: Black

BORDERS: Purchased school theme

LETTERING: Written with chalk

PROPS: "Bookshelf" wrapping paper; chalk; small school desk; doll or clothed stuffed animal; artificial apples; lunch box; books; web belt or book strap; small shelf; small blackboard; small posters with school room rules; adages; flag etiquette; small flag; toy school buses

INSTRUCTIONS: Fasten background to the walls. Fasten border around the top edges. Fasten the bookshelf paper across the bottom fourth of the walls. Attach a small shelf on the left wall. Write the title, childishly, with chalk across the upper third of the back wall. Staple posters to the walls, as if in a classroom. Fasten the flag to the top half of the left wall. Write on the "blackboard" walls like students would (draw a caricature of the teacher or principal; write simple math problems or "George + Dian" or letters of the alphabet). Put a small desk with the doll in it on the right side of the case. Arrange the lunch box, books, apples, and buses, around the case or on the shelf or desk.

TITLES:

Welcome Students Try Some "Holesome" Reading

Books Are "Holesome"

A Book A Day Keeps Illiteracy Away

BACKGROUND: Red

BORDERS: Purchased apples border

LETTERING: White pin backs and a purchased banner

PROPS: Large (two square feet) sheet of Styrofoam; knife; candle; red and green paint; books; T-pins; book slings

INSTRUCTIONS: Fasten the background to the board. Fasten the border around the edges. Fasten "Welcome Students" or "Welcome Back" banner across the top of the board. Cut an apple shape out of the Styrofoam (rub the knife blade on the candle to aid cutting). Cut out the center of the apple. Paint the apple red and leaves green. Pin the apple to the lower left side. Pin the title on the bottom right side of the board. Attach books to the board with slings.

TITLES:

Back To School With Reading

Read Back To School Books

Welcome Back To Books

BACKGROUND: Black or your school colors

BORDERS: Purchased red apple

LETTERING: White three-inch pin backs

PROPS: Felt in school colors or use red, white, and black theme; large sheet of Styrofoam; knife; candle; paint; T-pins; paint pens in coordinating color scheme; black marker

INSTRUCTIONS: Fasten the background to the board. Fasten the border to the edges. Cut apple shapes out of the Styrofoam (rub the knife blade on the candle to aid cutting) and paint shapes red. Use the above illustration for a pattern, if needed. Pin the apples to the bottom one-third of the board as illustrated. Staple the title to the middle of the board as shown. Make four pennants from the chosen colors in felt or poster board. Write the titles on them with paint pens and fasten them to the board as illustrated.

TITLES:

Books Add Color To Your Life

Color Your World With Reading

Reading Makes Your World Colorful

BACKGROUND: Black

LETTERING: Florescent green four-inch cutouts

PROPS: Large, inflatable crayons or large crayons made from poster board, foam board, or Styrofoam using the opaque projector; book titles written on smaller crayons (choose titles with colors in them or art books)

INSTRUCTIONS: Staple the background to the board. Add the border to the edges. Pin the large, inflatable crayons with pushpins through the hanger tab or tie fishing line around them and secure the fish line with T-pins. If you are using the poster board or Styrofoam crayons, simply staple or attach them with T-pins. Make smaller crayons (6 to 12 inches) using the die-cutter machine or just by drawing them, then cutting them out. You might use real crayons instead of making them. Scatter the smaller crayons around the board to add balance. Use a black marker to letter book titles with color words in the title on the smaller crayons or print titles on the computer, then cut them out and tape them to the crayons. Sample suggested titles are: *The Silver Dog; The Red Badge of Courage; The Scarlet Letter; The Yellow Room; A Solitary Blue; The Blue and the Gray; Fast Green Car; Anne of Green Gables.*

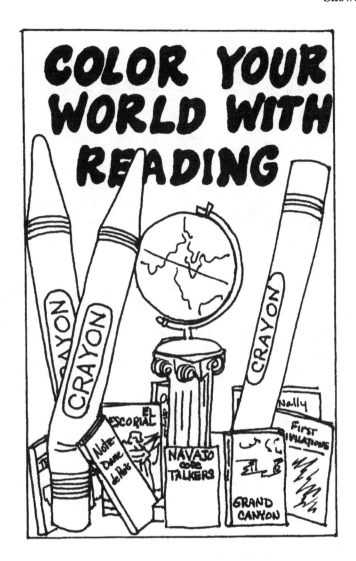

TITLES:

Color Your World With Reading

Colorful Reading

Colorful Books Make The World Go Round

BACKGROUND: Black

LETTERING: Purchased red, four-inch cutouts or die cuts

PROPS: Pedestal; world globe; three large, inflatable crayons or large crayons made from poster board or Styrofoam using the opaque or overhead projector; books about various cultures and countries of the world

INSTRUCTIONS: Staple the background to the walls of the showcase. Put the pedestal in the center of the floor with the world globe on top of it. Staple the title letters across the top third of the back wall. Arrange books standing up on the floor around the base of the pedestal. Place the inflated crayons, two on the left side of the globe and one on the right.

TITLES:

"Bag" 2 School Reading

"Bag" 2 Books

Welcome "Bag" 2 Books

BACKGROUND: Black or school colors

BORDERS: Red

LETTERING: Red four-inch cutouts

PROPS: Four shopping bags; tissue paper; school student handbook; school rule book; school procedure books and other pertinent beginning-of-the-year information; schedules; school calendar; T-pins or pushpins

INSTRUCTIONS: Staple the background to the board. Staple the border to the edges of the board. Write "Back 2 School" on the shopping bags. Use T-pins or pushpins to secure shopping bags to the four corners of the board. Center the title between the bags as shown. Put crumpled newspaper in the bags. Place co-coordinating tissue paper in the bags with some of it hanging out at the top. Place the school handbooks, schedules, calendars, and other appropriate back-to-school reading materials in the bags.

TITLES:

"Bag" To School Reading

"Bag" To The Library

"Bag" To The Books

BACKGROUND: Red

LETTERING: Yellow four-inch die cuts

FLOORING: Primary colors, crumpled tissue paper

PROPS: Nine primary colors shopping bags; primary colors tissue paper; books; newspapers

INSTRUCTIONS: Staple the background to the walls of the showcase. Staple and center the title in the upper half of the board as shown. Write "Back 2 School" on the shopping bags. Stuff the bags two-thirds full with crumpled newspaper. Place co-coordinating colored tissue paper in each bag with the ends sticking up and out of the bags. Make certain that the newspaper is covered by the tissue paper. Hang six of the shopping bags around the title and on the walls of the showcase. Place a book sticking up out of each bag with the title showing. Place three bags with books on the floor of the showcase as illustrated. Crumple various colored tissue paper around the bags in the floor of the showcase as illustrated.

TITLES:

Shopping For Good Back To School Reading

Back To Reading Buys

Shopping For Back To School Books

BACKGROUND: Red

BORDERS: Apple and ABC purchased border or solid apple green

LETTERING: White three-inch pin back

PROPS: Five brown paper sacks or sacks from various local bookstores; newspapers; books

INSTRUCTIONS: Staple the background to the board. Staple and center the title in the middle of the board as shown. Arrange the sacks around the title. Use T-pins and attach them firmly from the insides of the bags. Put scrunched up newspaper in the bags to make them stand out. Place the books in the bags protruding out so titles are easily read. Another suggestion is to use brown bags and write the titles and call numbers on the bags.

TITLES:

Shop 'Til You Drop For Back To School Books

Shopping For Back To School Books? Read These

Shopping For A Good Book? Try These

BACKGROUND: Yellow or school colors

LETTERING: Red, or co-coordinating school color, three-inch pin backs

FLOORING: Hardwood or carpet

PROPS: Toy shopping cart full of books; books; apples; rulers; back packs; large pencils; pens; notebooks; paper supplies; doll

INSTRUCTIONS: Staple background to the walls of the showcase. Staple and center the title to the upper back wall. Pin the notebooks and other school supplies on the side walls. Place the toy shopping cart filled with books about scholarships, the ACT, the SAT, study habits, and college selection or books on required reading lists in the left side of the showcase. Place the doll behind the cart, as if pushing it. Stack the other books and supplies on the right side of the toy shopping cart. Place artificial apples on the stacks of books and around the showcase floor to balance and fill in blank spots as needed.

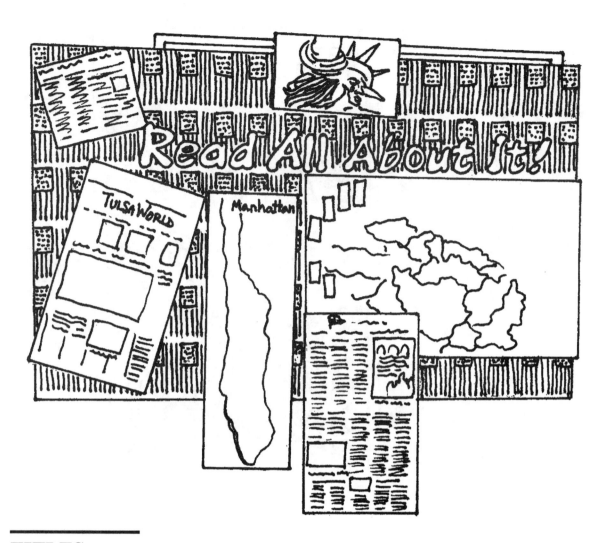

TITLES:

Read All About It!

In The News

Extra! Extra! Read All About It!

BACKGROUND: Flag material or solid blue

LETTERING: Black four-inch die cuts

PROPS: Maps of places of current conflict or current event sites; daily newspaper headlines; political cartoons and statements

INSTRUCTIONS: Staple the background to the board. Staple the title in the upper one-third of the board. Staple the maps to the board as illustrated. Staple daily newspaper reports about the events. This board may be adapted to any long-term news events such as the Olympics, the World Series, wars, and other happenings.

TITLES:

Revolutionary Reading

Revolutionary Books

Celebrate Constitution Week With Books

BACKGROUND: Red

LETTERING: Black four-inch cutouts

PROPS: Facsimiles of the Declaration of Independence, the Constitution, and the Articles of Confederation; posters dealing with the three branches of the government, preamble to the Constitution, and Bill of Rights; books; flag material; a Statue of Liberty poster, three-dimensional puzzle, or stand-up made from poster board using the opaque or overhead projector; Revolutionary War soldier dolls and other memorabilia

INSTRUCTIONS: Staple background to the walls of the showcase. Staple the title across the top of the board as shown. Build pedestals of different heights for dolls, puzzle or stand-up, and books, using books. Cover these books with flag material on the left side. Cover the other part of the floor of the showcase with solid blue material and pin the end of the material to the wall in the middle right side, as shown. Staple posters to the showcase walls as shown. Place the Statue of Liberty puzzle or standup on the tallest level in the left side of the showcase. Place the dolls and books about the Revolutionary War around the showcase floor as shown. Use slings to hang books on the walls.

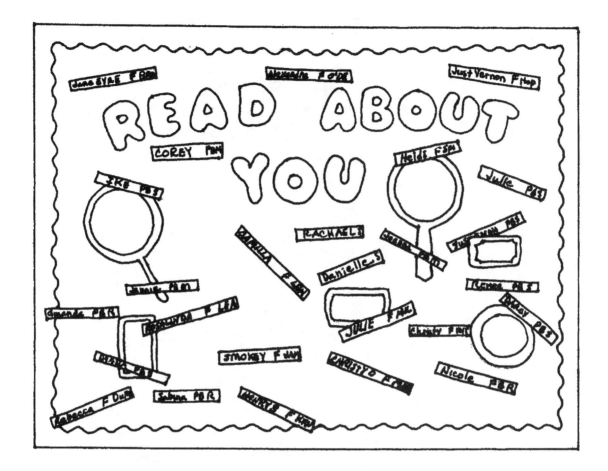

TITLES:

Read About You

Reading Reflections Of You

What's In A Name?

BACKGROUND: Green paper

BORDERS: Purchased plaid border

LETTERING: Red four-inch cutouts for "Read About" and black four-inch cutouts for "You"

PROPS: Construction paper in assorted colors; aluminum foil; book titles containing proper names either handwritten or computer generated; rubber cement

INSTRUCTIONS: Staple the background to the board. Staple "Read About" in a slight arch across the top of the board. Staple "You" in the center of the board below the other letters. Staple the border around the edges. Cut out a variety of mirror frame shapes in assorted colors of construction paper. Cut out foil "mirrors" to fit the frames and glue to frame shapes with rubber cement. Staple "name" book titles all over the board and across the mirrors, as shown.

TITLES:

Read About You

Reading Reflections

Reflective Reading

BACKGROUND: Striped wallpaper or wrapping paper

LETTERING: Black four-inch cutouts

FLOORING: Wood

PROPS: Large mirror; four medium mirrors; books with proper names in their titles; toy mirrors; small or miniature mirrors; bookends

INSTRUCTIONS: Staple the background to the board. Hang or lean the large mirror on the back wall. Hang other mirrors on the walls. Use bookends to make two groups of books stand up on both sides of the mirror. Select books that contain student names or the word "mirror" in the titles. Lay miniature mirrors and compacts around the floor of the showcase to fill blank spaces and add balance.

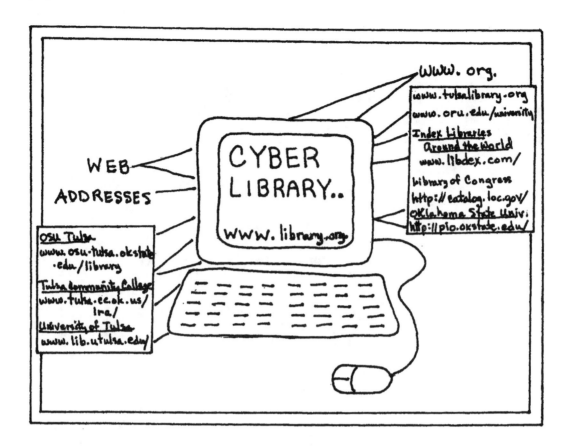

TITLES:

Cyber Library

Cyber Books

Cyber Reading

BACKGROUND: Navy blue or black

LETTERING: White three-inch pin backs or cutouts

PROPS: Red thin ribbon; large computer made from foam core poster board using the opaque, overhead, or document camera projectors; two lists of usefulWorld Wide Web addresses and organizations

INSTRUCTIONS: Staple background to the bulletin board. Make a large computer (almost as tall as your bulletin board) by using the above illustration on the opaque, overhead, or document camera projector. Trace the computer on foam core board, Styrofoam, or poster board. Cut out the computer and staple or T-pin it to the center of the board. Use pin back letters to pin the title slogan on the computer screen. Prepare two lists of outstanding and useful Web sites. Staple one of the lists to the top right. Staple the other list to the bottom left. Use the red ribbon to make web lines from the lists to the computer as illustrated. Suggestions for Web sites are www.libdex.com, Index of Libraries around the world; www.tulsalibrary.org, Tulsa County Library; www.oru.edu/university/library, Oral Roberts University Library; http://catalog.loc.gov/, Library of Congress; www.osu-tulsa.okstate.edu/library, OSU Tulsa Library; http://libraries.ou.edu/, University of Oklahoma Libraries; http://www.odl.state.ok.us/, Oklahoma State Department of Libraries. Sites' addresses are accurate as of publication date.

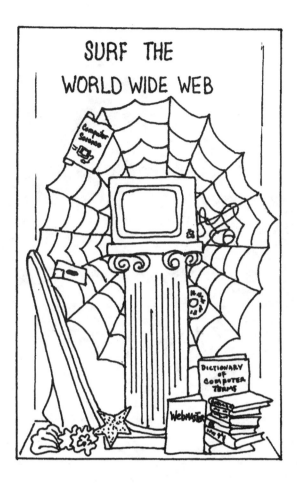

TITLES:

Surf The World Wide Web

Surf The Net

Don't Get Caught In The Web...Read

BACKGROUND: Black garbage bags

LETTERING: White four-inch cutouts

FLOORING: Sand paper

PROPS: Fishing net or large spider web or several small spider webs or white string or yarn to make a world wide web; surfboard, boogie board, or other surfing type equipment; sea shells; beach items; sea creatures; star fish; column; small computer or a poster board cutout of a computer (purchased or constructed); books

INSTRUCTIONS: Staple the background to the walls of the showcase. Pin a large spider web or fishnet on the back wall as shown. A web can be made by going from top to bottom and side to side using white string or yarn and pushpins. The pushpins are used to hold each point in the web in place. Staple the title approximately one-third from the top. Line the bottom of the showcase with sandpaper. Place the column in the center of the showcase. Place a small computer monitor, nonworking laptop, or child's toy computer in the center of the column. Place a stack of books about the Internet on the right side of the bottom of the showcase. Lean the surfboard or boogie board in the left corner of the showcase. Place seashells and other beach items randomly around the floor of the showcase and in the net to fill in blank spots.

TITLES:

Grooovy Books, Man

The '60s Were Grooovy, Baby!

Hippie Days

BACKGROUND: Tie-dyed laminated napkins or solid fluorescent colors

LETTERING: Black four-inch cutouts

PROPS: Peace signs; books; slings; enlarged drawing of a hippie head; beads; sunglasses; daisy cutouts

INSTRUCTIONS: Staple the background to the board. Center the title in the top of the board. Staple the hippie head, centered, in the bottom half of the board as shown. Staple the peace signs, daisies, beads, and other '60s memorabilia around the title and top half of the board. Use slings to hang '60s-type books in the bottom half of the board around the head.

TITLES:

Grooovy Books, Baby!

Man! The Library Has Groovy Books!

Be Hip! Read!

BACKGROUND: Tie-dyed patterned wrapping paper or fabric or party napkins

LETTERING: Red four-inch cutouts

FLOORING: Wood or existing showcase floor

PROPS: Peace signs; smiley faces; books about the '60s; clothes and jewelry from the '60s; large poster of Austin Powers, or a hippie; heavy cardboard or poster board; yardstick; flower pot full of sand or gravel; glue; tape; pushpins; rubber cement; artificial daisies

INSRUCTIONS: Tape napkins together and laminate, or use wrapping paper or fabric and fasten to the walls. Staple the title irregularly across the top third of the back wall, as shown. Cut out the Austin Powers figure from the poster. Glue the figure to cardboard or poster board, then cut it out. Tape a yardstick to the back of the figure and push the end into a pot of gravel. Place the stand-up figure in the middle left showcase floor. Cover the pot with tie-dyed material or colorful fabric. Surround the stand-up figure with books about the '60s. Hang '60s vintage clothing, such as a jumpsuit or mini dress, from the walls of the showcase. Hang love beads and other jewelry around the clothing to enhance the overall appearance. Add peace signs and smiley faces, putting some on the showcase glass with a dot of rubber cement. Scatter daisies and other objects around the showcase floor to achieve balance.

TITLES:

Reading Is The Best D (section of a real mini fence) *Against Illiteracy*

D-fence Against Ignorance = Read

Books Are The Best D-fence For Literacy

BACKGROUND: Navy blue or school colors

LETTERING: White three-inch pin backs

PROPS: Small section of plastic fence (sold in most garden shops); Styrofoam sheet; knife; candle; red paint; purchased poster figures of a football referee (and cheerleader, if desired); megaphone picture; school "spirit ribbons"; T-pins; pompon; reading list

INSTRUCTIONS: Cut a large (approximately 12 inches) letter D from the Styrofoam sheet (rub the knife on the candle to make cutting easier). Paint the D red or a contrasting color of choice. Hang the fence section on T-pins across the center of the board toward the right. To the left of the fence, pin the D. Fasten the title down the center, using "D-fence" in the center. Fasten the referee in the upper left corner, the megaphone in the upper right, the cheerleader or pompon in the lower right, and the reading list in the lower left. Spirit ribbons can be added along the sides and bottom.

TITLES:

Kick Off The Year With Sports Books

Get A Kick Out Of The New Books

Get A Kick Out Of Books (feature joke and riddle books)

BACKGROUND: School team colors

LETTERING: Contrasting school color three-inch pin backs or four-inch cutouts

FLOORING: Artificial turf with fall colors painted on and mixed with the green turf

PROPS: Stuffed large doll, or large stuffed animal (be creative and use a stuffed animal mascot, for example, a bear if the team is named the Bears); dress the character in a football jersey and helmet or a jogging suit and football shoes; football or Styrofoam football cutout painted like a football (could also use a poster board or die-cut football); books about football and other sports; school pennant; spirit ribbon; green strip of grass background; megaphone

INSTRUCTIONS: Staple the background to the walls of the showcase. Staple the green grass strip around the base of the walls of the showcase. Fasten the dressed figure to the back wall of the case with T-pins, pushpins, or staples. Arrange the legs so that they appear to be kicking the ball as illustrated. A football could be partially deflated and hung on the wall. A Styrofoam football could be cut out and pinned to the wall as shown. Stack the books on the right side of the showcase floor. Staple the title above the figure. Staple a school pennant above the title. Hang a spirit ribbon on the right wall. Place a megaphone on top of the stacked books as shown. Add more spirit ribbons and school buttons, and hang sports books, using slings, as desired to balance out the showcase.

TITLES:

Celebrate Hispanic Heritage Month

Add A Bit Of Salsa To Your Reading

Salsa Reading

BACKGROUND: Green, white, and red (Mexico's flag colors cut in three or equal size vertical strips) or red and yellow for the Spanish flag

LETTERING: Black three-inch pin backs

PROPS: Newspaper and Internet articles about the heritage month celebrations, Hispanic heroes, and noted celebrities; biographies and photos of famous Hispanics; colored construction paper; green, red, and white kraft paper cut in three equal strips to fit the board in one-third vertical sections; flags of all South American countries; glue stick; large sombrero

INSTRUCTIONS: Dividing the board into three equal vertical parts, staple the green paper on the left side, then the white, and then the red to simulate Mexico's flag. Make or purchase small flags of Hispanic countries. These flags are very simple to make from construction paper. Photocopy the covers of the biographies and cut them out. Staple the title across the top of the board. Fasten everything else around the board as illustrated. Attach the sombrero to the upper right corner of the board, overlapping onto the wall, if desired.

TITLES:

Research Hispanic Heritage Month

Explore Hispanic Heritage Month

Hispanic Heritage Month...Read About It!

BACKGROUND: Green

LETTERING: Black three-inch pin backs

FLOORING: Wood

PROPS: Sombrero; serape; God's eye; Mexican doll; donkeys; birds; other Hispanic memorabilia; books; castanets

INSTRUCTIONS: Staple the background to the walls. Attach the title to the upper middle of the back wall. Hang a serape with a sombrero at the top as shown. Center and hang the God's eye under the title. Stack approximately 15 books in the right corner. Place a donkey or other memorabilia on top of the books. Place books on the left side as shown. Hang a set of castanets above the books. Place donkeys, dolls, and other items around the books and floor of the showcase to achieve balance and eye appeal.

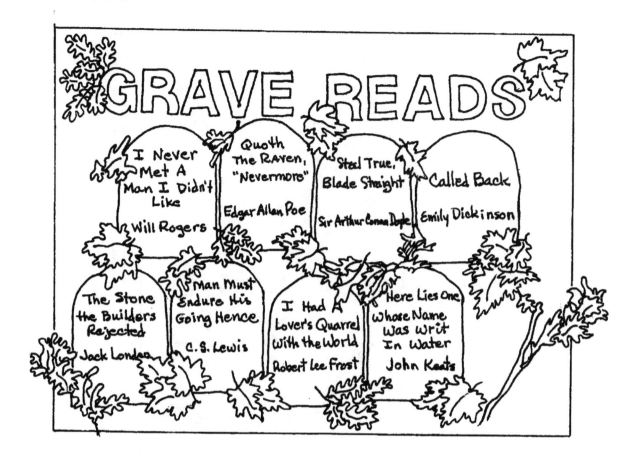

TITLES:

Grave Reads

Grave Readings

Tombstone Tales

BACKGROUND: Black

BORDERS: Black or none

LETTERING: Laminated aluminum foil four-inch die cuts

PROPS: Eight Styrofoam tombstones made from sheets of Styrofoam or they may be purchased; knife; candle; autumn leaves; epitaphs from author tombstones; gray paint; brush; overhead transparency sheets; T-pins

INSTRUCTIONS: Staple background to the board. Staple the title across the top. Trace the tombstones (freehand or use opaque, overhead, or document camera to transfer a pattern to the Styrofoam). Rub the knife against the candle to make cutting the Styrofoam easier. This process may need to be repeated often since you are making several tombstones. Cut out the tombstones. Paint the tombstones gray. Copy epitaphs of famous authors onto transparency sheets. Fasten sheets to the tombstones with straight pins; then fasten the tombstones to the board with T-pins by pushing T-pins through all the layers. Staple the autumn leaves around the board, at the base and tops of the tombstones, and around the title.

TITLES:

R.ead I.n P.eace

Moonlight Madness Books

Read By The Light Of The Moon

BACKGROUND: Black

LETTERING: Painted or written with a black marker

FLOORING: Artificial turf with dabs of earth tone paints

PROPS: Tree branch; autumn leaves; black and orange construction paper; large piece heavy corrugated cardboard; plastic fence section; black paint; black marker; utility knife or heavy scissors; paint brush; small stuffed animals or beanbag animals; book catalogs; Halloween theme books or scary books; clear tape; bat shape

INSTRUCTIONS: Staple the background to the showcase back and walls. Place turf on the floor. Cut out an orange paper moon and a black paper bat. Staple them to the background as shown. Place the tree limb in the right side of the showcase, leaning toward the left. Attach autumn leaves to the tree limbs and showcase walls and ceiling. Cut a large piece of cardboard into a tombstone shape. Cut two smaller tombstones of different sizes. With a black marker, write the title on the large tombstone, outline and fill in the larger letters with paint. On one of the smaller tombstones write this or a similar epitaph: "Here Lies Illiteracy / Done in by a conspiracy / Of plots so bewitching / Students can't be resisting." On the other small tombstone write "Jack Dawson...." This is the fictional hero of the movie *Titanic* and brought numerous students into the library to read about the Titanic. Paint the fence section black. Place the tombstones across the back of the showcase floor, behind the fence and the tree limb. Scatter books, leaves, and stuffed animals around the floor, on the limb and on the fence. Fashion small books from pictures cut out of the publisher catalogs and tape them to the animals' paws.

TITLES:

D (imprint of feet) *Illiteracy Read*

D (imprint of feet) *Illiteracy—Read Daily*

D (imprint of feet) *Bad Grades—Use Your Research Skills*

BACKGROUND: Black

LETTERING: 12-inch red foam letter D; two 10-inch feet; orange four-inch cutouts

FLOORING: Autumn-colored carpet, green carpet, or burlap

PROPS: Tree limb; tombstones; fence section; witch in a chair; models of spiders; spider webs; fluorescent purchased six-inch feet; leaves

INSTRUCTIONS: Staple the background to the back showcase wall. Place the turf on the floor. Place the tree in the middle of the showcase. Staple the title to the back showcase wall as shown. Staple the large pair of feet as shown. Lean and attach cardboard tombstones next to the tree on both sides. Place the fence in front of the graveyard scene. Set the witch in the right corner in front of the fence. Place a fictional witch book in her hands. Place various books in front of the fence. Place the spiders on the books, in the tree, and on the title as shown. Scatter leaves around the bottom of the showcase as desired.

TITLES:

Prevent Brain Rot! Read!

Prevent Illiteracy...Read

Don't Be Brain Dead! Read!

BACKGROUND: Black

LETTERING: Red four-inch cutouts

PROPS: Tree limb; artificial turf; autumn leaves, corn stalks; plastic skulls and bones; cardboard or Styrofoam tombstone; black paint or marker

INSTRUCTIONS: Staple the background to the walls. Build up the bottom of the case with books. Place the "tree" in position and cover the base with the turf. Paint the tombstone gray and write an epitaph about illiteracy in black. Scatter bones and leaves throughout the display. Put stalks near the back wall.

TITLES:

Mystifying Mummy Tales

Mummifying Reading

Wrapped Up In Mysteries

BACKGROUND: Black

BORDERS: Orange

LETTERING: Four-inch orange cutouts

PROPS: Two dolls (approximately the same size); muslin; a book list about mummies and mysteries

INSTRUCTIONS: Staple the background to the board. Staple the border to the board. Center and staple the title in the upper half of the board as shown. Tear or cut the muslin into two-inch strips. Wrap the dolls in strips of muslin to make them look like mummy dolls. Attach one doll on the left side of the title and one on the right side. Attach a book list in the bottom center of the board.

TITLES:

Get Wrapped Up In Reading

Mummifying Mysteries

Books Wrap Me Up!

BACKGROUND: Black

LETTERING: Three-inch white pin backs

FLOORING: Black trash bags

PROPS: Doll or inflatable skeleton; old sheet or muslin torn into two-inch strips; tree limb; orange paper moon; Spanish moss; tombstone; mystery and/or horror books

INSTRUCTIONS: Staple the background to the sides of the showcase. Stack old books for a seat for the mummy. Cover these books and floor with black trash bags. Place the tree limb on the left side of the showcase. Staple the moon behind the tree. Pin the title on the background so it is visible through the tree limbs. Make a tombstone from cardboard and label "R.ead I.n P.eace." Paint the edges of the tombstone to look aged and made of stone. Wrap the inflatable skeleton or doll in the strips of an old sheet or muslin so it looks like a mummy. Seat the mummy on the covered books with a book in its hands or lap. Arrange other books around the scene. Drape the display with Spanish moss as shown.

TITLES:

Monster Mania Reading

Monster Mash Book Bash

Monster Books

BACKGROUND: Black

BORDERS: Pumpkin garland or solid orange

LETTERING: Four-inch orange and black cutouts

PROPS: Halloween masks of monsters and creatures such as Dracula, a werewolf, Frankenstein, Phantom of the Opera, a Jason hockey mask, a Scream monster mask, and so forth; large spiders and bugs; books featuring these monsters and creatures; slings; fishing line; miniature books (made from publishers' catalogs)

INSTRUCTIONS: Staple the background to the board. Staple the pumpkin garland or orange border to the board. Staple the title in the upper third of the board. Pin the masks around the board as desired. Tie the spiders and bugs to fishing line. Suspend them down the board by tying them to paper clips and hooking the clips behind the board. Use slings to hang books on the board as needed to balance the board. Cut miniature books from publishing catalogs and glue them to cardstock. Tape miniature books to the legs of the small spiders.

TITLES:

Monster Mash Book Bash

Scream About Reading

Reading's A Scream

BACKGROUND: Orange

LETTERING: Four-inch cutouts

FLOORING: Artificial turf (painted in fall colors)

PROPS: Halloween masks or costumes (Phantom of the Opera, Jason hockey mask, and the Scream ghost or whatever strange creatures you have or find in seasonal sales); fall leaves; raffia; slings; horror books; hangers; black garbage bags; black hats

INSTRUCTIONS: Staple the background to the showcase wall. Put fall-colored artificial turf in the showcase floor. Staple the title in the top half of the board. Bend hangers into an oval shape. Tape or attach masks to cover the hangers to make the monster faces. Tie fishing line to the top of the hangers. Cut a small hole in the bottom of a black garbage bag. Put the bag on the hanger and under the mask. Cut jagged edges at the bottom of the black garbage bag. Repeat this process for the other monsters. Suspend these monsters from the showcase ceiling. Staple autumn leaves around the title, showcase walls, and floor. Place books randomly around the floor. Scatter raffia and leaves around the books to add texture to the showcase.

TITLES:

Best "Witches" For Bewitching Books

Bewitching Books

Best "Witches" For "Spooktacular" Books

BACKGROUND: Black

LETTERING: White three-inch pin backs

PROPS: Witch dolls or faces; leaves

INSTRUCTIONS: Staple the background to the board. Depending on how many witches used and the size of the board, the arrangement will vary. The featured board places one witch at the left top and one on the right side. Attach the title as shown in the middle of the board. Scatter and staple fall leaves around the board.

TITLES:

Note To Self: "Learn To Read!"

Out Of Control Reading

Control Your Life, Read!

BACKGROUND: Black

LETTERING: Computer generated

PROPS: Tree limb; purchased witch kit (or make one with a hat, wig, cape, broom, fake hands, shoes, and socks); autumn leaves; plastic bones and skull; cardboard or Styrofoam tombstone; gray paint; black paint or markers; yellow paper; wooden ruler; ghost template for die-cut machines; two good-sized rocks

INSTRUCTIONS: Paint the tombstone gray. Write an epitaph to illiteracy on the tombstone with black paint or marker. Place the tree limb in position on the left side of the showcase. Fasten the witch on top of the tree as shown. Cut the poster board into a cartoon balloon shaped title with "thought bubbles" and staple to the back wall, as if it were the witch's thought. Print "tree ahead" diagonally on the yellow paper; cut it into a traffic warning sign. Tape the sign to the ruler and anchor between the rocks at the base of the tree. Cover the floor of the showcase with leaves. Prop the tombstone against the lower right corner of the case. Put a skull and bones by the marker. Print illiteracy statistics on white paper and cut them into die-cut ghost shapes. Staple these ghosts. Put leaves on the limb.

TITLES:

The Price Of Freedom Is Visible Here

Monumental Reading

National Monuments Reading

BACKGROUND: Royal Blue

BORDERS: Purchased flag border

LETTERING: White three-inch pin backs

PROPS: Flags; flag stickers; photos of the Vietnam Veterans Memorial, Tomb of the Unknown Soldier, Arlington National Cemetery, Korean War Veterans Memorial, *U.S.S. Arizona* Pearl Harbor, Marine Corps Memorial Flag Raising at Iwo Jima, World War I Memorial, Cemetery Ridge Gettysburg, or other monuments

INSTRUCTIONS: Staple the background to the board. Staple the border to the edges. Attach and center the title in the top one-third of the board. Staple the photos randomly around the board as shown. Place the flag stickers around the photos to add balance.

TITLES:

Veteran's Day Reading

Veteran Reading

Give Thanks For Freedom

BACKGROUND: Royal blue or red

LETTERING: Blue four-inch cutouts

FLOORING: Royal blue fabric and flag fabric

PROPS: G.I. Joe and Barbie dolls in war-related clothing and uniforms or photos of soldiers in the Civil War, the War of 1812, the Spanish American War, World War I, World War II, Korean War, Vietnam War, Gulf War, and the War Against Terrorism; flags; books; weaponry; plant stand; books

INSTRUCTIONS: Staple the background to the back wall of the showcase. Put the plant stand or other objects to elevate and section off the showcase into different historical eras of war. Cover the bottom of the plant stand and floor of the showcase with blue material on the left and the flag material on the right. Place books about the various wars in the back of each section. Place the photos or dolls in action poses in front of the books about their war. Add nurses of the time period and Rosie the Riveter doll and informa-tion. Use slings to place books on the walls. Add articles from newspapers or information found in other sources on the walls and around the dolls as shown.

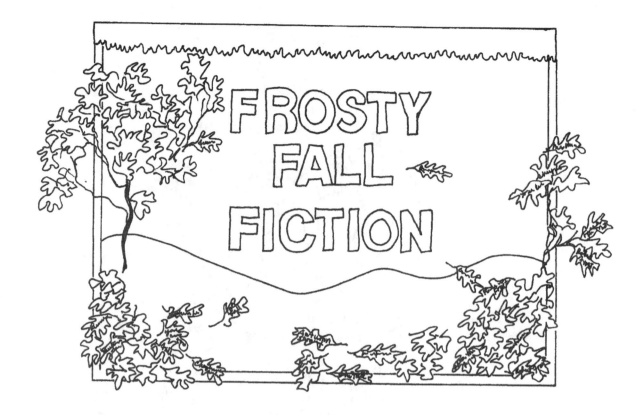

TITLES:

Frosty Fall Fiction

Fall Into Fiction

Fall For Books

BACKGROUND: Blue for top two-thirds and green felt for the bottom one-third of the board

BORDERS: Purchased icicle border

LETTERING: Four-inch laminated aluminum foil die cuts

PROPS: Purchased branches of autumn leaves; loose leaves with book titles printed on them; green felt; white or gray net

INSTRUCTIONS: Staple the background to the board. Staple the border across the top edge. Cut the felt into a "hill-shaped" strip about one-third of the board's height and cover with netting for a frosty look. Staple this netting and felt across the bottom third of the board as shown. Center and staple the title in the center top portion of the board. Attach autumn leaf branches to each side of the board. Write autumn titles of books on the leaves and scatter them across the bottom portion of the board.

TITLES:

Sweater Weather Reading

Fall Reading

Sweater Weather Books

BACKGROUND: Sky blue computer paper with a cloud design

LETTERING: Four-inch red die-cut letters or red pin back letters

PROPS: Assorted sweaters in children's or doll sizes; a school sweater if available; artificial autumn leaves; popular books with an autumn theme; pushpins; clear tape

INSTRUCTIONS: Tape computer sheets in lengths to fit the showcase back and sides (be sure they will fit in the laminating machine) and laminate. Staple to the back and sides of the showcase. Staple the title to the upper back of the showcase. Use pushpins to attach the sweaters to the back and sides of the showcase. Put the artificial turf on the showcase floor. Position the sleeves to "hold" the books as shown, allowing the books to be supported by pushpins as well as the sleeves. The pins may be used inside the sweaters for a more attractive appearance. Arrange additional books on the floor of the showcase and leaning on the sides. Staple the leaves to the sides and back. Attach leaves to the ceiling with staples, pins, or tape. Drop leaves randomly over the display.

TITLES:

Pilgrim Tales

Pilgrim Yarns

Be Thankful For Books

BACKGROUND: Dark blue

LETTERING: White four-inch cutouts

PROPS: Pilgrim dolls; fall leaves; pumpkins (real or artificial); ornamental corn; husks; gourds; books; pieces of hay or raffia

INSTRUCTIONS: Staple the background to the board. Center and staple the title to the upper one-third of the top. Staple the Pilgrim dolls in the center of the board. Staple fall leaves, pumpkins, ornamental corn, and hay around the Pilgrims' feet. If real pumpkins are used, attach them to the board with T-pins. Use slings to attach seasonal books on the sides of the showcase and other appropriate places.

TITLES:

Pilgrim Plots

Pilgrim Fiction

Read About The Pilgrims

BACKGROUND: Dark blue

LETTERING: White four-inch cutouts

FLOORING: Fall-colored artificial turf

PROPS: Pilgrim dolls; miniature bales of hay; fall leaves; ceramic pumpkins; ornamental corn; husks; gourds; small alphabet blocks that spell "Happy Thanksgiving"; books about Thanksgiving and pilgrims; bench; branches of autumn leaves; corn stalks

INSTRUCTIONS: Staple the background to the walls. Place turf on the showcase floor. Place the small bench in the center with a mini hay bale on each end. Place dolls sitting on the hay bales. Fasten the branches and leaves behind the bench and up the walls as shown. Put corn stalks behind the dolls. Arrange a book display on the bench and floor. Stack blocks on the floor to spell out the greeting. Place ornamental corn on the bench and floor.

TITLES:

Seasonal Books Light Up Your Life!

Light Up Your Holidays, Read!

Seasonal Books Are Enlightening

BACKGROUND: Red

BORDERS: Holly

LETTERING: White three-inch pins

PROPS: Eight feet of artificial pine garland; eight two-inch red tree ornaments; black marker; T-pins; two-inch gold or silver star; string of large bulb tree lights; ornament hangers

INSTRUCTIONS: Staple the background and border to the bulletin board. Attach the title to the right half of the board. Use T-pins to arrange and attach the pine garland in a zigzag method to create a tree shape. String lights over the garland, hooking them on the pins. Fasten the star to the top of the tree. Write seasonal book titles on the ornaments with a marker and hang them on the tree.

> **Variation:** A string of battery-powered small lights may be used. However, these were found to burn out in one day and then did not show up on the tree. The large bulb lights are visible even when off.

TITLES:

Shed Light On The Holidays

Seasonal Books Light Up Your Life

Seasonal Reading

BACKGROUND: Red

LETTERING: White four-inch cutouts

PROPS: Top section of an artificial tree, or a small tree; poster board; 10-inch wreath; small tree ornaments; tea light candles; books about Hannukah, Advent, holiday customs, Kwanzaa, *The Night Before Christmas,* and other holiday themes; markers; T-pins; hot glue gun; book slings

INSTRUCTIONS: Staple the background to the board. Staple the title down the center of the board. Decorate the tree, and then pin it to the upper left corner. Draw a menorah and Kwanzaa candelabra on poster or foam board and color it with markers. Cut them out and staple to the board as illustrated. Glue four tea lights onto the wreath, then pin the wreath to the bottom of the board, beneath the title. Hang holiday books near the appropriate "light" (Jewish book by the menorah, Advent by the wreath, etc.).

TITLES:

These Books "Sleigh" Me!

Sleigh Full Of Reading

Sleighing Reading

BACKGROUND: Dark blue

LETTERING: White four-inch cutouts

PROPS: Sleigh (made using the opaque, overhead, or document camera projectors); poster board, foam board, or Styrofoam; snowflakes; humorous books; cotton batting or stuffing for snow mounds

INSTRUCTIONS: Staple the background to the board. Center and staple the title to the upper one-third of the board. Attach the sleigh to the bottom left of the board. Use white stuffing or batting to make snow drifts around the sleigh and bottom of the board. Attach humorous books or book jackets in the sleigh. Staple the snowflakes onto the blue background as illustrated.

TITLES:

Sleigh Bells Ring Are You Readin'?

Sleigh Full Of Reading

Sleigh Full Of Books

BACKGROUND: Dark blue

LETTERING: White four-inch cutouts and two-inch pin backs or cutouts

FLOORING: White cotton batting

PROPS: Old books or boxes to build up the base of the showcase; white cotton batting; large plastic or cardboard snowflakes; a sleigh that will fit into the showcase; lacing; about 30 five-eighths-inch jingle bells; artificial holly and poinsettia blooms; four or five two-inch jingle bells; 12 inches of two-inch-wide red ribbon; assorted small toys; holiday or Christmas books, preferably with a "bell" or "ring" in the title; straight pins; fishing line

INSTRUCTIONS: Staple the background to the walls of the showcase. Create a slope or hillside effect with old books or small boxes and cover it with cotton batting. Staple the title to the back wall. Cut a point on one end of the two-inch ribbon and fold under one-half inch on the other end. Staple the folded end of the ribbon to the back wall next to the beginning of the title. Use pins to attach large jingle bells to the ribbon. Thread the smaller jingle bells on a length of lacing and knot the ends. Drape the string of bells from the front of the sleigh to the back. Put the sleigh in position in the showcase and arrange books and toys inside. Decorate it with holly and poinsettia blossoms. Arrange other books in the snow. Hang snowflakes from the showcase ceiling with fishing line and staple snowflakes to the walls.

> **Variation:** The slope could be made to represent a rooftop with a chimney using corrugated "brick" paper and black construction paper shingles. Cotton batting pieces and spray snow complete the effect.

TITLES:

Grinchy Reading

'Tis The Season To Be Reading

Grinch Time Reading

BACKGROUND: Red

BORDER: Christmas light string, large bulb variety

LETTERING: Green four-inch die cuts

PROPS: White poster board; red "brick" corrugated paper; Christmas greenery; gift-wrap bow; light-weight holiday ornaments; holiday books; picture frame with a portrait; stuffed Grinch doll in a Santa suit; red drawstring gift bag; pushpins; T-pins; newspaper or tissue paper

INSTRUCTIONS: Staple the background to the board. Staple the title across the top of the board. Drape the string of lights on pushpins across the top of the board, letting it hang down the sides. Cut a rectangle of brick paper for the fireplace and hearth. (Cut a firebox and draw or cut out a "fire" to put in it.) Staple it to the board. Cut a long rectangle of white poster board for the mantel. Staple it to the top of the fireplace. Staple the greenery to the mantel. Decorate the greenery with ornaments hung on pushpins. Hang a framed portrait over the mantel. Attach the Grinch doll to the left of the fireplace, using T-pins. Staple the gift bag near the doll's feet, then place the string in the doll's hand. Stuff the bag with tissue or newspaper. Put books sticking out of the bag. Hang books with slings on the side of the fireplace. Staple the greenery to the right of the fireplace in a tree shape.

TITLES:

Grinchy Reading

Don't Be A Grinch, Read!

Grinchy Books

BACKGROUND: Green

BORDERS: Gold and silver garland

LETTERING: Red four-inch cutouts

FLOORING: Wood

PROPS: Grinch doll; Cindy Lou Who doll or other small doll; dog stuffed animal; little pine tree; red velvet Santa pack; corrugated brick fireplace; green, gold, and silver garland; miniature log basket and twigs; books about the holiday season; holiday photos; small books, pine cones, miniature clock, and so forth for the mantel; small stockings

INSTRUCTIONS: Staple the background to the showcase walls. Use corrugated brick paper and create a fireplace. Place the fireplace in the right side of the showcase. Pin the Grinch doll in a standing position to the left corner wall. Place the Cindy Lou Who doll and the dog doll in front of the fireplace. Pose them looking at the Grinch. Place a small pine tree on the bottom right side. Put the miniature log basket filled with twigs in front of the fireplace next to the tree. Hang seasonal pictures on the back and side walls as shown. Staple the title at the top of the back wall. Place the books and miniature clock, pinecones, and other items on the mantel. Drape green garland across the fireplace. Hang gold and silver garland at the top of the showcase and hang it down both sides. Hang stockings from the fireplace.

TITLES:

Holidaze Books "Mint" To Be Read

Books "Mint" To Be Read

You Were "Mint" To Read

BACKGROUND: Red

BORDERS: Purchased red-and-white candy cane border

LETTERING: Red-and-white striped wrapping paper die-cut letters

PROPS: Six-inch Styrofoam circles; red acrylic paint; plastic wrap; strips of paper printed with holiday book titles with a candy theme (for example, *The Candy Cane Caper)*; real candy canes or cutouts of candy canes; T-pins; clear tape

INSTRUCTIONS: Staple the background to the board. Staple the title across the entire board in a staggered fashion as illustrated. Paint red wedges on the Styrofoam circles to simulate peppermint candies; wrap the "mints" in plastic wrap to complete the candy look. Tape the book titles onto the wrapped mints. Attach the candies to the board with T-pins through the twisted plastic wrap. Staple the candy cane cutouts in spaces on the board. If you are using real candy canes, either tape them to the background or hang them on T-pins.

TITLES:

Holidaze Books "Mint" To Be Read

Read Down Candy Cane Lane

Holiday Books "Mint" To Be Read

BACKGROUND: Blue

LETTERING: Red four-inch cutouts

FLOORING: Cotton batting

PROPS: Two six-inch Styrofoam circles; plastic wrap; red paint; two-foot plastic candy canes with bows; cotton batting; brown kraft paper; books with "sweet" titles or holiday cookbooks; old books or boxes; strips of paper with "sweet" book titles; T-pins

INSTRUCTIONS: Staple the background to the showcase walls. Staple the title across the top third of the back wall. Stack old books or boxes to build up the floor of the showcase in graduating levels. Make a "lane" down the levels with brown paper. Drape cotton batting on both sides of the pathway and over the base of books or boxes to form a snowy slope. Poke the ends of the canes through the batting, wedging them into the base to line the "lane." Paint the Styrofoam circles with wedges of paint to make "mints." Wrap with twists of plastic wrap. Tape the book title strips onto the "mints." T-pin the mints to the wall by the showcase title. Place holiday books along the pathway.

TITLES:

Sleddin' Readin'

Slide Into Reading

Sledding Books

BACKGROUND: Blue for the sky and white for the mountain

LETTERING: Three-inch white pin backs

PROPS: Sleds; stuffed animals (bears, Grinch, rabbits, etc.)

INSTRUCTIONS: Staple the blue background to the board. Staple the white paper hillside in place as illustrated. Attach the title slanted above the white snow strip. Attach sleds (real or created on the opaque, overhead, or document camera projectors) to the snow background. Attach the stuffed animals to the sleds. Pin miniature books to their paws or tape book titles to the sleds. Staple the snowflakes as illustrated.

TITLES:

Snuggle Up With Winter Reading

Warm Winter Reading

Dreaming Of Winter Reading

BACKGROUND: Green and gold brocade wrapping paper or wallpaper

LETTERING: Green or black four-inch die cuts

FLOORING: Small rug or quilt

PROPS: Fireplace made from red corrugated brick-patterned paper with a white poster board mantel; small sticks or logs for the fire; black paper for back of fire box; flame picture; chair and doll; library/book printed wrapping paper; miniature books; small picture frame; small animals; books; small basket with twigs in it

INSTRUCTIONS: Staple the background and title to the showcase walls as shown. Staple a strip of book wrapping paper around the bottom walls to look like bookcases. Place a chair on the left side of showcase. Place the fireplace against the back wall, slightly to the right of center. Put miniature books and photo frame on the mantel of the fireplace. Place the wood in the firebox and tape the "flames" behind it, if desired. Put the small rug or quilt on the floor and arrange small animals "reading" miniature books. Place the basket of twigs and library books to the right of the fireplace. Place a doll in the chair and add books around her chair and one in her lap.

TITLES:

Read And Melt The Winter Away

Melt The Winter Away With Reading

Don't Have A Meltdown! Read!

BACKGROUND: Blue

LETTERING: White four-inch die cuts or cutouts

PROPS: White cotton batting; old top hat or any real or plastic hat for a snowman; two small round pieces of Styrofoam; black paint; stuffed cloth carrot or a real one; two small tree or shrub branches; book with "winter" or "snow" in the title; newspapers or white paper; T-pins

INSTRUCTIONS: Staple the background to the board. Staple the title across the upper half of the board as shown. Make a ball of crumpled paper and cover it with cotton batting. Pin it to the board below the left end of the title. Cut two round circles from Styrofoam. Paint them black. Use them for the snowman's eyes. Pin the black "eyes" onto the snowman head; pin on the carrot for the nose. Staple the batting across the bottom of the board and in a mound around the snowman's head as shown. Fasten the sticks as arms. Fasten one of the books in an open position between the sticks.

TITLES:

Don't Have A Meltdown! Read!

Read The Winter Away

Melt The Winter With Heart Warming Books

BACKGROUND: Blue

LETTERING: White four-inch cutouts

FLOORING: Stack of books covered with cotton batting

PROPS: Snowflakes; top hat; white trash bag; newspapers; cotton batting; charcoal or chunks of Styrofoam painted black; carrot or stuffed fabric carrot; branched twigs for arms; books with "snowy" titles; wire coat hangers; wire cutters; fishing line

INSTRUCTIONS: Staple the background to the walls. Staple the title across the upper half of the back wall. Mound old books or boxes on the showcase floor and cover with some of the batting. Stuff the bottom portion of a trash bag with crumpled newspaper. Drape with more batting and place on top of the snow mound, tucking the "neck" in a little to define a head. Poke a little hole for the carrot nose and coal eyes. Place the coal buttons on the melting body. Stick the twigs into the snow and scatter books around the display. Put the hat on top of the head. Cut lengths of a coat hanger to fit snugly across the top of the showcase. Hang snowflakes from them using the fishing line as illustrated.

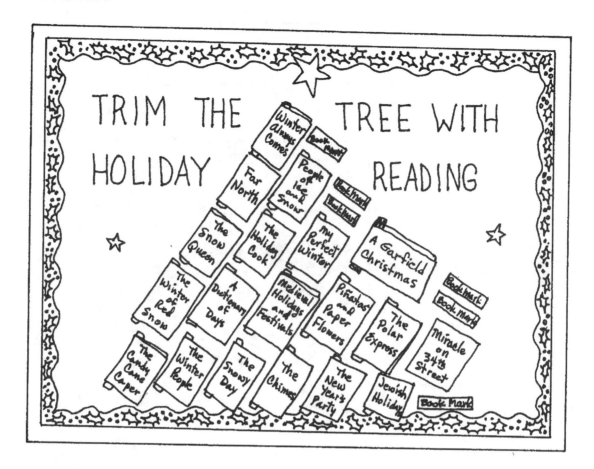

TITLES:

Trim The Tree With Holiday Reading

The Reading Tree

Tree Time Reading

BACKGROUND: Red

BORDERS: Purchased holly border

LETTERING: Three-inch white pin backs

PROPS: Large star; books; small stars; bookmarks; slings

INSTRUCTIONS: Staple the background to the board. Staple the border to the edges of the board. Place the title at the top as shown. Using book slings, create a tree from paperback and hardback holiday books as illustrated. Place small stars and bookmarks around the board as needed to balance the display.

TITLES:

Nutcracker Reading

Classic Holiday Reading

Christmas Fantasies

BACKGROUND: Red

LETTERING: White two-inch pin backs

FLOORING: Carpet

PROPS: White lace curtain panel and tie-back; large toy soldier, soldier doll, or use opaque or overhead projector to make a poster board picture, using the illustration as a pattern; two tall gift-wrapped boxes; Sugarplum Fairy Barbie or other ballerina doll; Nutcracker Ken or other male doll in costume; mouse stuffed toy; small crown; swords for doll and mouse; holiday and Christmas-theme books; green poster board or kraft paper; various colors of construction paper; pushpins

INSTRUCTIONS: Staple the background to the walls of the showcase. Staple the title, centered, about one-third of the way down the back wall. Cut a tree shape from the green poster board or kraft paper. Decorate the tree with ornaments cut from the construction paper. Staple the tree, centered, in the lower portion of the back wall. Place a wrapped box on each side of the showcase floor. Put the toy soldier on one of the boxes and the ballerina doll on the other. Lean books against one of the gifts. Stack two or three books in front of the box on the right and place the mouse on top of them. Put the crown on the mouse's head and a sword in his hand, making him the "Mouse King." Place the nutcracker beside the gift on the left, sword in hand. Fasten the curtain panel across the inside top front of the showcase with staples or pushpins. Pull the panel to the left and drape it gracefully, using the tie-back and pushpins. Make sure the title is visible before fastening.

TITLES:

Ring In The New Year With Reading

Ring In The School Year With Reading

Ring In Books

BACKGROUND: Yellow

BORDERS: Solid red

LETTERING: Red four-inch cutouts

PROPS: Poster of the head and shoulders of a large, typical, in-style student; large notebook "rings" through the nose, ears (have at least three in each ear, the more the better, the students loved it), and eyebrow; bangle bracelets would be useful; necklace of 12 rings; reading list of books on tattoos and body piercing

INSTRUCTIONS: Staple the background and border to the board. Using an opaque or overhead projector, draw the outline of the student; cut out and color it. Pierce the poster with notebook rings in the ears, eyebrows, and nostrils. Make a necklace of the 12 rings and hang it around the neck. Firmly staple the poster head to the board (the rings make it heavy). Staple the title as shown. Make a reading list of books about tattoos, body piercing, and so forth. Staple it to the board as shown.

TITLES:

Virus Gotcha Down? Read!

Debug Your Brain, Read!

Bugged By Books

BACKGROUND: Lime green tissue paper, taped together and laminated

LETTERING: Purple four-inch cutouts

PROPS: Plant stand; old computer monitor; keyboard; computer parts; eight one-inch-thick, four-inch-diameter Styrofoam circles; various colors of sparkly one-inch poms; various colors of sparkly chenille craft sticks; green floral sticks (remove wires); the tractor feed margins torn from computer paper in long, connected strips, if available; computer printouts; diskettes; assorted paints and a brush; enlarged computer cartoon; straight pins

INSTRUCTIONS: Staple the background to the walls. Staple the title to the top one-third of the back wall. Set the plant stand (or small tables or stacks of computer oriented books) in the showcase. Arrange scrap computer parts on all surfaces; place the monitor on the top level. Paint Styrofoam circles gray or silver with brightly colored spots. Pin the poms on top of each circle for "eyes," then poke chenille sticks in for antennae. Push three or four floral sticks into the underside of the circles to serve as legs. Push large floppy computer discs into the side of the Styrofoam circles to make wings for the "bugs." Place bugs among the computer parts and attached to the side walls. Drape strips of computer tractor feed paper over the props.

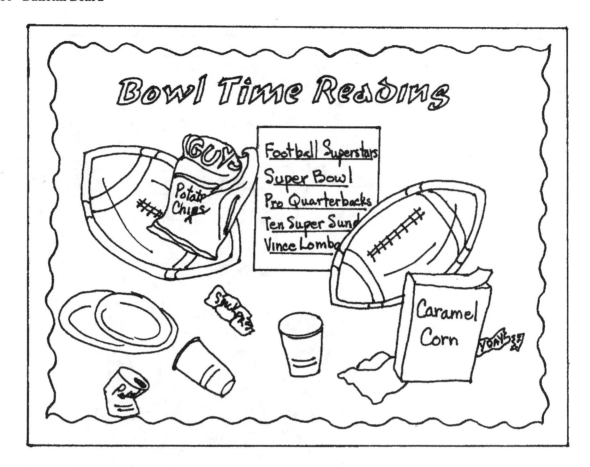

TITLES:

Bowl Time Reading

Game Day Books

Bowl Time Books

BACKGROUND: Royal Blue

BORDERS: Purchased football border or solid gold border

LETTERING: Gold four-inch die cuts

PROPS: Two large plastic bowls that look like footballs or large shallow snack plastic bowls; potato chip bags; empty soda cans; empty caramel corn box; Styrofoam cups; candy bar wrappers; paper plates; napkins; list of football books; football bowl game information from the Internet

INSTRUCTIONS: Staple the background to the board. Staple the border to the edges. Staple the title to the top of the board. Center and staple the reading list under the title. Use T-pins to attach the plastic football snack bowls as shown (one on the left of the list and one at the bottom right of the list.) Staple the empty popcorn box and candy wrappers to the bottom right of the board. Attach the Styrofoam or paper cups, paper plates, soda cans, and candy wrappers to the board as shown. An additional feature could be information about all the college bowls printed from the Internet and stapled to the board.

TITLES:

Super Bowl Reading

Super Bowl Super Reading

Super Bowl Book Alert!

BACKGROUND: Kelly green

LETTERING: Black four-inch die cuts

FLOORING: Wood

PROPS: Bowl game information from the Internet; pedestal; large punch bowl or large plastic bowl; footballs; pompons; books about the Super Bowl and pro football teams; slings

INSTRUCTIONS: Staple the background to the walls. Staple the title to the top of the board. Center and place the pedestal in the showcase. Place the large bowl on the pedestal. Place the footballs, books, and pompons in the bowl. Use slings to hang books on the walls of the showcase. Add a football on either side of the pedestal on the showcase floor. Place the pompons around the bottom of the showcase.

TITLES:

Prevent "Crack Ups"—Read The Signs!

Don't Be A Dummy, Read!

Know How To Read The Signs

BACKGROUND: Yellow

LETTERING: Red four-inch cutouts

PROPS: Crash test dummies sitting in a car (use the above illustration for the pattern); titles of driver's education books; stop signs, yield signs, one way signs, and so forth; driver's manual; poster board; markers; construction paper

INSTRUCTIONS: Staple the background to the board. Make two crash test dummies sitting in a car using the opaque, overhead, or document camera projectors. Staple the dummies to the board as shown. Use construction paper or poster board to make traffic signs. Kits for these signs can sometimes be found in school specialty stores. Staple the title in the top one-third of the board. Staple traffic signs around the board as illustrated. Use a sling to hang the driver's manual in the upper right corner. Make a balloon slogan sign on the computer that states: "Even dummies know enough to buckle up!" and attach it above the top of the car.

TITLES:

Don't Be A Sucker! Read!

Even Suckers Read

Reading Is For Everyone, Even Suckers!

BACKGROUND: Yellow

LETTERING: Green four-inch die cuts

PROPS: Large Styrofoam six-inch circles; two-inch balls; real Tootsie Pops® or various other candy suckers; small Dum Dums® for bookmarks in books; books; colored plastic wrap

INSTRUCTIONS: Cover the Styrofoam balls with colored plastic wrap to look like suckers. Use dowel rods or sticks (from trees, spray painted white) for sucker sticks. Staple the background to the walls. Staple the title as shown. Staple or pin suckers haphazardly around the title. Add book titles to the suckers or type the titles on the computer and add them to the showcase walls. Add books standing at the bottom of the showcase. Put Dum Dum® suckers in these books for the bookmarks. Staple Tootsie Pops® and other suckers around the showcase walls and floor to complete the visual effect.

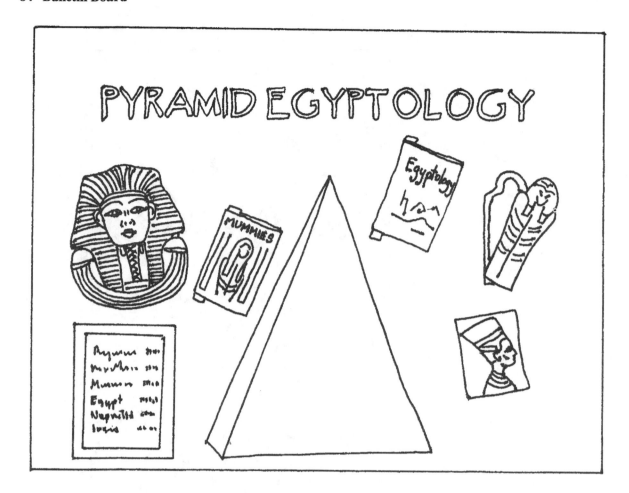

TITLES:

Pyramid Egyptology

Book A Trip To The Pyramids

Classic Egyptian Reading

BACKGROUND: Turquoise

LETTERING: Beige or gold four-inch cutouts

PROPS: Posters of King Tut, Nefertiti; mummies; sphinx; any colorful items about the pyramids or Egyptology; large pyramid made from gold laminated wrapping paper or beige poster board; slings; books; reading list

INSTRUCTIONS: Staple the background to the board. Staple the title to the top of the board. Make a large pyramid from laminated gold wrapping paper or beige poster board. Center and staple the pyramid under the title. Staple photos of Egyptian scenes, kings, and queens (clipped from old magazines or from Internet sources) around the pyramid. Use slings to hang Egyptology books from the board as shown. Staple the reading list to the lower left corner.

TITLES:

Peer-Amid Great Books

Pyramid Egyptology

Peer-Amid The Classics

BACKGROUND: General pale or "sandy" appearance

LETTERING: Two different colors of construction paper to coordinate with background, four-inch die cuts

FLOORING: Sand or sandpaper

PROPS: Pyramid of gold paper (could use brown paper); illustration of an Egyptian mummy scene taped to the pyramid; map of Egypt; small mummy cases made from a purchased kit; King Tut mask, perhaps one made by an art student; books; covers; illustrations; sand or sandpaper

INSTRUCTIONS: Use the die-cut machine to cut the title letters into two colors and overlap them when stapling them to the board. Thumbtack the pyramid to the board by reaching up inside the bottom of it. If using other props, fasten them to the showcase back wall and sides. Put down sand or sandpaper for the showcase flooring. Put Egyptian themed books around the display, along with any other "artifacts" you can borrow or find in garage sales and clearance sales.

TITLES:

We've Got "Male" Reading

We've Got "Fe-mail" Reading

Macho, Macho Man Books (omit use of mailbox with this title)

BACKGROUND: White or pale blue

LETTERING: Black four-inch cutouts; red four-inch cutouts for "male"

PROPS: Poster board cutout in the shape of a mailbox with its flag up and an envelope sticking out appropriately painted or colored; computer printout from your library's electronic card catalog with a reading list with synopses of male-oriented books; posters of men playing sports or reading

INSTRUCTIONS: Staple the background to the board. Staple the title as shown. Staple the mailbox in the upper left quadrant. Attach the reading list on the upper right. Pin posters across the bottom of the board. If using the "fe-mail" alternate title, make the same board for female-oriented books.

TITLES:

Female Reading

Female Sports Books

Female Scholarship Books

BACKGROUND: Brick corrugated paper

LETTERING: Black four-inch die cuts

PROPS: Opaque projector-produced window with a girl reading, or use a doll reading; miniature balls (soccer, basketball, football, softball); books about corresponding sports; swim goggles; corrugated brick patterned paper

INSTRUCTIONS: Cut a strip of brick paper four inches wider than the showcase. Bend back two inches on each end and staple it to the walls, making a ledge in front of the archway, so that the girl appears to be sitting on the ledge. Staple a picture of the archway to the back wall. Staple a "brick" wall around it all the way to the floor, and around the sides. Stand sports books across the showcase floor, balancing the appropriate miniature ball on top of each book. Put the swim goggles in front of or on top of a swimming book.

TITLES:

Just An Old-Fashioned Love Story

Heart Time Reading

February Sweetheart Reading

BACKGROUND: Black

BORDERS: Purchased "candy hearts" print

LETTERING: Red two-inch pin backs

PROPS: Large, empty heart-shaped candy box; bouquet of artificial roses wrapped in green florist tissue and tied with ribbon; red and pink die-cut hearts with love story book titles written on them; thumbtacks

INSTRUCTIONS: Staple the background and border to the board. Thumbtack the bottom of the empty candy box to the upper left corner, then replace the cover. Tack the bouquet to the lower right corner. Pin the title in the center of the board. Surround the title with book-titled hearts.

TITLES:

Romantic Knights

Knightly Romance Reading

Good Knights For Reading

BACKGROUND: Gold and green brocade wrapping paper or wallpaper

LETTERING: Black four-inch cutouts

FLOORING: Wood

PROPS: Two metal knights or two knights made from poster board using the opaque or overhead projector to reproduce the above illustration; female doll with a long skirt or dress; ivy garland; books; pedestal; fabric

INSTRUCTIONS: Staple the background to the showcase walls. Staple the title in the upper one-third of the board. Place the doll in the middle of the showcase on the pedestal. If the doll's dress doesn't cover the pedestal, drape it with fabric to create a long skirt effect. Place one knight on the left side of the doll and the other knight on the right. Place a book in the doll's hands. Stand romance books in front of the knights and doll. Hang the ivy garland at the top of the showcase as illustrated.

TITLES:

Famous Sweethearts Hang Out At The Library

Undying Love Stories Hang Out In The Library

Famous Sweethearts Hang Out In The Library

BACKGROUND: Black

LETTERING: Red four-inch cutouts

PROPS: White heart doilies; smaller red paper hearts with famous lovers' names written on them; one- to two-inch-wide red ribbon; glue; black marker

INSTRUCTIONS: Staple the background and border to the board. Staple the title down the center portion of the board, as shown. Cut lengths of ribbon as illustrated, trim the ends decoratively. Glue red hearts onto the doily hearts and write couples' names on them with a black marker. Staple these hearts to the doilies. Suggestions for names: Romeo & Juliet; Jane Eyre & Rochester; Heathcliff & Catherine; Hamlet & Ophelia; Cinderella & Prince Charming; Napoleon & Josephine; Roy Rogers & Dale Evans; Elizabeth & Robert Browning; Scarlett O'Hara & Rhett Butler; Daisy & Gatsby

TITLES:

Famous Lovers Hang Out In The Library

Undying Love Hangs Out In The Library

Hang Out With Famous Sweethearts In The Library

BACKGROUND: Black satin or gold-flocked wallpaper or wrapping paper

BORDERS: None

LETTERING: Red three-inch pin backs

PROPS: Four clothes hangers; 22 six-inch valentines; romance books; gold bookends; 10 yards of red one-inch ribbons, string, or fishing line

INSTRUCTIONS: Staple the background to the walls of the showcase. Cut the ribbon in lengths appropriate for the individual showcase. Tie, glue, or staple the ribbon to the hangers as shown. Leave approximately the same amount of space between the valentines to create a balanced effect. Use T-pins or pushpins to hang the hangers. Add books around the showcase floor as desired to fill the blank spots. Letter the valentines or print out names on the computer and then glue them to the valentines. Suggestions for names of famous sweethearts are: Romeo & Juliet; Heathcliff & Catherine; Eliza Doolittle & Professor Higgins; Helen of Troy & Paris; Charlie Brown & the Red-Headed Girl; Scarlett O'Hara & Rhett Butler; Tom Sawyer & Becky Thatcher; Aladdin & Jasmine; Ricky & Lucy Ricardo (Arnez); King Arthur & Guinevere & Lancelot; Daisy & Gatsby; Jane Eyre & Rochester; Hamlet & Ophelia; Napoleon & Josephine; Adam & Eve; Elizabeth & Robert Browning.

TITLES:

Lonely Hearts Club

Lonely Hearts Reading

Books For Lonely Hearts

BACKGROUND: Pink

LETTERING: Black two-inch pin backs

PROPS: Large red paper heart with a smaller heart cut out of the center; silk flowers and greenery; red construction paper hearts; large and small markers

INSTRUCTIONS: Staple the background to the board. Center the largest heart and staple it. Pin the title within the opening. Pin and staple the flowers and greenery in the top and around the bottom of the heart. Write romance titles on the larger construction paper hearts. Staple them downward on the right and left sides of the board. Staple the small hearts all over the remaining space. Variation: Cut the largest heart out of a one-inch-thick Styrofoam sheet. Paint it red and fasten it to the board with T-pins. Rubbing a knife blade on a candle makes it easier to cut Styrofoam.

TITLES:

Read About A Legend

Legendary Reading (Biographies)

Legendary Books

BACKGROUND: Red

BORDERS: Black or none

LETTERING: A sign with titles and information about the biography section

PROPS: Posters and photos of famous legends (this one used Marilyn Monroe, Elvis Presley, and James Dean)

INSTRUCTIONS: Staple the background to the board. Arrange photos and posters as illustrated or desired. Place the title in the upper right corner of the board.

TITLES:

Read Any Good Books Lately?

Unsinkable Reading

Unsinkable Romances

BACKGROUND: Navy or dark purple; white paper or Styrofoam "shoreline" strip

LETTERING: White three-inch pin backs

PROPS: Poster board; movie poster or drawing made with opaque or overhead projector; white book tape; reading list of good books

INSTRUCTIONS: Staple the background to the board. Staple the "shoreline" about one-third from the top. If you are using a movie poster, staple it to the left side of the board. If making the scene, use poster board to make the railings. Make a cartoon "bubble" with the white tape, then pin the title inside the bubble. Staple the reading list at the end of the railing. Small chunks of Styrofoam can be used to simulate icebergs and ice floating in the ocean.

TITLES:

Titanic Reading

The Ability To Read Makes You Unsinkable

Unsinkable Books

BACKGROUND: Black

LETTERING: Silver four-inch die cuts

FLOORING: Wood

PROPS: Three-tiered plant stand; model of the *Titanic*; *Titanic* memorabilia; books about the *Titanic*; seashells

INSTRUCTIONS: Staple the background to the showcase walls. Staple the title in the upper one-fourth of the showcase. Place the plant stand or stacks of books to make different heights in the showcase. Place the *Titanic* model on the highest level of the stand. Place the books and *Titanic* memorabilia around and on the plant stand and floor of the showcase. Scatter seashells and starfish around the floor, on top of the books, and other areas as needed.

TITLES:

Read About Black History In February

Pioneers Of Black History

Biographies Of Great Black Leaders

BACKGROUND: Red

BORDERS: Purchased valentine border

LETTERING: White three-inch pin backs and a "Black History" banner

PROPS: Posters and photos of honored African American leaders; biographical information about African American leaders; purchased banner for Black History or draw one using the opaque projector or overhead projector

INSTRUCTIONS: Staple the background to the board. Staple the border to the edges of the board. Pin the title in the upper middle of the board with the banner in the center. Staple the photos and posters with biographical information around the board as shown.

TITLES:

Book A Trip To The Orient

Explore The Mysterious Orient

Oriental Reading

BACKGROUND: Oriental print or Oriental flower patterned wallpaper

LETTERING: Computer-generated or handmade sign with the title lettered on it

PROPS: Artificial ivy vines; plant leaves and butterfly; large folding paper fan; Oriental lantern; Oriental souvenir doll; travel posters; T-pin or pushpins; books about the Orient

INSTRUCTIONS: Staple the wallpaper to the walls. Staple the travel posters to the back wall. Staple the title sign in the center of the wall on top of the posters. Pin the butterfly in a space by the title. Pin the vines across the top and down the side walls. Hang the lantern on the left side. Open the fan and prop it on a book on the floor. Cover the book base and floor with fabric or a kimono. Place books about the Orient around the floor and leaning on the walls. Put a souvenir doll or other travel souvenirs in the display. Arrange the plant leaves among the books.

TITLES:

March Madness

March Madness Reading

March Brings Basketball Madness

BACKGROUND: School colors or any solid color

BORDER: Newspaper or contrasting school color

LETTERING: Red four-inch punch outs

PROPS: College pennants made from construction paper or purchased; basketball made from poster board or purchased; small toy basketball goal made to hang on a door; cardboard basketball players; NCAA tournament brackets from the newspaper or Internet

INSTRUCTIONS: Staple the background to the board. Staple the border on all sides. Attach the basketball goal/net by hanging the door clip over the top of the bulletin board. Place the college pennants of local teams in the NCAA tournament on the edges of the bulletin board. Highlight empty spaces with cardboard basketball players and ball. Before long, the board will be covered with articles. Brackets are updated after each round to heighten interest about who is going to be in the Final Four.

TITLES:

Reading Hoops

Jump Into Reading

Jump Into Basketball Books

BACKGROUND: Black

LETTERING: Red four-inch die cuts

FLOORING: Wood

PROPS: Basketball books; toy basketball goal; basketball; pennants; spirit ribbons; large basketball shoes; T-pins

INSTRUCTIONS: Staple the background to the walls of the showcase. Staple the title in the upper left of the showcase as shown. Use T-pins to attach the toy basketball goal in the upper right of the showcase. Hang pennants and spirit ribbons on the side walls. Use slings to hang books on the back wall. Stack books in the right floor of the showcase. Place a basketball on top of this stack of books. Place a pair of large basketball shoes on the floor of the showcase as shown. Place one or two books in the goal.

TITLES:

Wonder Women! (March Is Women's History Month!)

Wonderful Women

Women Suffragettes

BACKGROUND: Any solid color

BORDER: Metallic gold or a contrasting color

LETTERING: Metallic gold paper or same color as the border, four-inch die cuts or cutouts

PROPS: Copies of pictures of leaders of the women's suffrage movement (can be taken from encyclopedias, posters, or biographies); inexpensive mats or "frames" made from a paper with a design in coordinating colors; typed or printed questions about and clues to the identities of the women; gold or yellow star cutouts; sign stating: "March Is Women's History Month!"; timeline of the suffrage movement

INSTRUCTIONS: Staple the background to the board. Staple the border on all sides. Staple the title in the center of the board as shown. Type questions and/or clues about each woman under her picture and "frame" the pictures and captions. Staple the framed pictures around the right side, top, and bottom of the board. Staple the sign over the upper right corner, projecting off the board. Staple the timeline down the left side as shown. Comments: Examples for this board would be a picture of Elizabeth Cady Stanton with the caption "Who was Susan B. Anthony's partner for the right of women to vote?" then, a picture of Susan B. Anthony with the caption "Who was the first woman to have her image on a U.S. coin and why?"

TITLES:

Women Of Wonder

Read About Heroines

Valiant Women Reading

BACKGROUND: Yellow

LETTERING: Red four-inch cutouts or die cuts

FLOORING: Carpet or none

PROPS: Column; Wonder Woman figure cut from a poster or made using the opaque or overhead projector and poster board; Styrofoam block; glue; T-pins; long strip of white paper; black marker; books about famous women who have made an impact on history and society

INSTRUCTIONS: Staple the background to the walls. Staple the title in the upper left corner. Make an "honor roll" of famous women, using the marker and white paper, then staple it to the left back wall below the title. Put down the carpet, if using it. Glue the Styrofoam block to the back of the figure in the body area. Push two T-pins into the wall where you want the body attached, then push the figure and block onto the pins. This will anchor the figure to the wall. Place the column next to the figure. Stack books on top of the column until the figure's hand can rest on the top book. Lean other books against the base.

TITLES:

Read And The Force Is With You

FORCE-ful Reading

Sci-Fi Books

BACKGROUND: Black

BORDERS: Gold

LETTERING: Gold four-inch cutouts

PROPS: *Star Wars* masks

INSTRUCTIONS: Staple the background and border to the board. Staple the title to the center of the board. Hang *Star Wars* masks on either side of the title.

TITLES:

Eggstra Terrestrial Reading

Eggstraordinary Reading

Eggsceptional Books

BACKGROUND: Blue with clouds or light blue

LETTERING: Springtime colors four-inch die cuts

PROPS: Large springtime-colored plastic or poster board eggs; artificial (Easter basket type) green grass; green burlap; alien stuffed animal; books

INSTRUCTIONS: Staple the background to the showcase walls. Staple the title in the upper one-half of the showcase as shown. Build up the showcase floor with mounds of newspapers. Cover the newspaper with the green burlap and green grass. Place the eggs in the center of the grass. Place the alien doll sitting on the middle egg. Tape a book to the doll's hands so he looks like he is reading. Use slings to attach science fiction books to the showcase walls. Place several books in the grass as desired.

TITLES:

Blooming Tales

Blooming Books

Books Make You Bloom

BACKGROUND: Light blue

LETTERING: Hot pink four-inch cutouts

PROPS: Three large and six to eight small tissue paper or silk flowers; grass strip cut from green kraft paper; butterflies, either purchased artificial ones or handmade from construction paper; green kraft paper "leaves" for the flowers; marker

INSTRUCTIONS: Staple the background to the board. Staple the title in the upper one-third of the board. Staple the grass strip across the bottom of the board. Tuck the stems behind the grass strip. Then attach the smaller tissue or silk flowers around the large flowers. Put the stems behind the grass strip and staple them in place. Write the book titles on the leaves, then staple them to the stems. Using a marker, make little dots onto the background to suggest a butterfly's flight. Fasten one butterfly to the "end" of this "flight." Staple other butterflies around the board, on flowers and grass.

TITLES:

"Wooden Shoe" Like To Read A Romance?

"Wooden Shoe" Love To Read New Books?

"Wooden Shoe" Want To Read About Holland?

BACKGROUND: Blue sky with white clouds (wrapping or computer paper taped together and laminated)

LETTERING: Black three-inch pin backs

FLOORING: Green artificial turf

PROPS: Enlarged computer-generated windmill laminated and cut out (or a small windmill that will fit into the display case); wooden shoes; artificial tulips; romance books; old books or boxes to build up the base of the display

INSTRUCTIONS: Staple the background to the walls of the showcase. Build different levels in the showcase with old books or boxes and cover with the turf. Staple the windmill to the right back wall. Fasten the title to the back wall to fit around the windmill as shown. Arrange shoes, books, and tulips in an inviting display.

TITLES:

Prom Time Reading

Prom Time Books

Prom Time Fiction

BACKGROUND: Navy blue

LETTERING: White four-inch die cuts

PROPS: Crescent moon cut from yellow paper; silhouettes of boy and girl cut from black paper; bridge made from poster board (make girl, boy, and bridge by using an opaque or overhead projector); free-form "river banks" cut from green paper; aluminum foil stars; booklist of romances, prom, or dance books; books about school dances or proms; slings

INSTRUCTIONS: Staple the background to the board. Center and staple the title at the top. Staple the moon left of the title. Staple the boy and girl in the middle of the board, then staple the bridge on top of them, so that they appear to be standing behind the railing. Staple the green banks at both ends of the bridge. Staple the book list under the bridge, then use slings to hang books on each side of the board. Staple stars around the sky as shown.

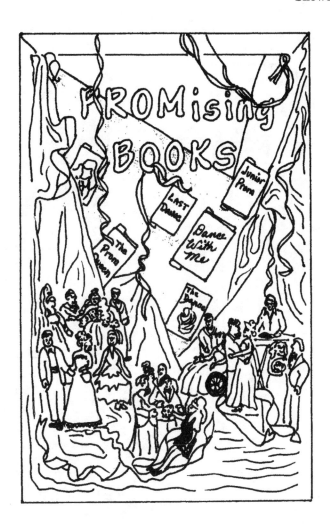

TITLES:

PROMising Books

PROMising Fiction

PROMising Reading

BACKGROUND: Colors chosen for the prom theme

LETTERING: Coordinating color with the background colors four-inch die cuts, "ising" in lower case

PROPS: Solid color wrapping paper; fabric and ribbons in the prom colors; male and female fashion dolls in prom attire (try to feature as many ethnic groups as possible; also try to feature dolls with different body types, e.g., heavyset, thin, short, and tall as well as dolls with physical disabilities); books with "prom" or "dress" in the titles; old books or boxes; slings

INSTRUCTIONS: Staple large strips of wrapping paper at angles to the walls of the showcase, covering the entire surface. Build up the base with old books or boxes to make various levels. Drape the base with different prom colored fabrics, stapling them to the walls to create a backdrop. Staple the title to the upper portion of the back wall. Hang books on the back wall below the title. Arrange the dolls (as many as available) in groups on the various levels. If possible, get a wheelchair figure and a DJ doll with accessories. It is not necessary for each doll to have "dates"; uneven numbers are good and realistic. Staple, hang, and drape the ribbon around and in the display.

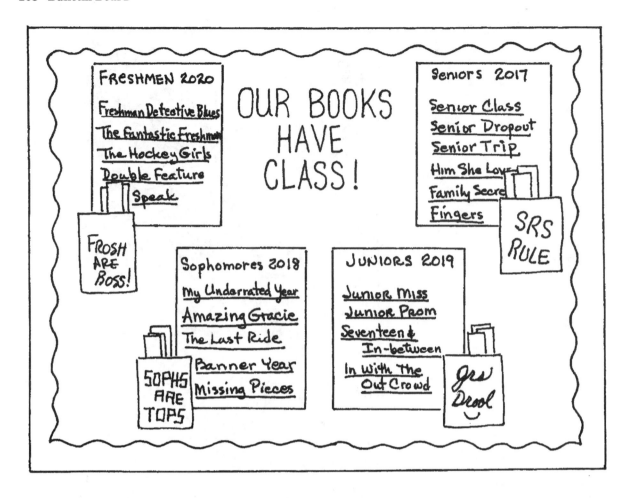

TITLES:

Our Books Have Class

Classy Books

Classy Classics

BACKGROUND: Your school color

BORDERS: Your other school color

LETTERING: Three-inch white pin backs

PROPS: Four reading lists, one for each class; slogans about each class; four five-by-seven-inch manila envelopes with the top end cut off; glue

INSTRUCTIONS: Staple the background and then the border to the board. Make four lists (one for each class in school) of books about each age group with and/or titles including the words, "freshman," "sophomore," "junior," and "senior," if possible. Title the lists for each class with their graduation year. Make reduced copies of the lists for the students to take. Staple an envelope at the bottom of each reading list. Glue the appropriate slogan on the envelope. Put reduced copies of the lists in the envelopes.

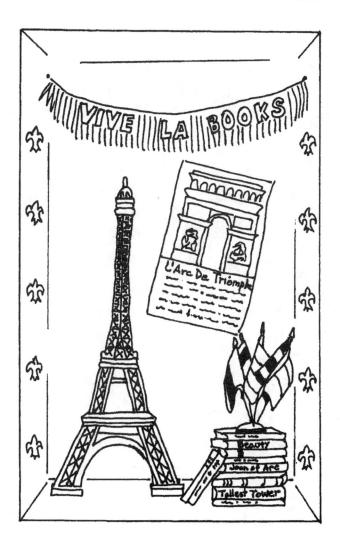

TITLES:

Vive La Books

Vive La French Heritage

Vive La Library

BACKGROUND: Royal blue

LETTERING: White four-inch cutouts

FLOORING: Artificial turf or none

PROPS: Model, three-D puzzle, a cutout made from poster board, or a poster of the Eiffel Tower; French travel poster; red paper or a purchased party banner; gold fleurs-de-lis; French flag or a collection of flags from the French regions; books about France and the French; glue; pushpins

INSTRUCTIONS: Staple the background to the walls. Make a long fringe banner from red paper, or use a purchased party banner. Glue the title letters to the fringe. Hang the banner across the upper part of the showcase, using pushpins. Staple the travel poster, at an angle, to the right part of the back wall. Staple the fleurs-de-lis down each side wall. Place the tower on the left side of the showcase. Stack and arrange books on the right. If using a flag set, put the flags on top of the books. If using only a French flag, make some sort of stand for it, maybe using a Styrofoam block.

TITLES:

Rise And Shine! It's Reading Time

Puppy Dog Tales

Rise And Whine! It's Reading Time

BACKGROUND: Wallpaper for a baby's room or in solid light yellow or mint green

LETTERING: Black three-inch pin backs

PROPS: Six stuffed puppies (or any stuffed animals approximately the same size); Styrofoam lengths or poster board to make a baby bed; baby hats; paperback books; baby bottles; pacifiers; bibs

INSTRUCTIONS: Staple the background to the board. Use Styrofoam or poster board to make a white baby bed as shown. Put baby hats on the stuffed animals. Attach the animals in a row with T-pins. Pin strips of Styrofoam or poster over the stuffed animals. Staple the title in the upper part of the board. Attach pacifiers and baby bottles around the board as illustrated.

TITLES:

Garden Of Readin'

Garden Of Fiction

Plant Your Reading Garden

BACKGROUND: Blue sky with white clouds (computer paper or wrapping paper)

LETTERING: Black three-inch pin backs

FLOORING: Earthy artificial turf and Spanish moss

PROPS: Artificial turf that has been daubed with brown and orange paint to look earthy; computer-generated garden and field with barn, enlarged and joined to form scene; craft sticks for fence; tree limb; toy garden tools; "half" basket; books; Spanish moss; small pictures of books cut from catalogs; "'Lettuce' Read!" sign made from colored paper; rubber cement

INSTRUCTIONS: Staple the background to the walls of the showcase. Laminate the scene and staple in place. Fasten the craft sticks to the scene with rubber cement to make a fence. Put the turf on the floor. Place the tree limb on the right side of the showcase. Put the half basket on the left side and fill the basket with books. Place more books around the base of the tree. Arrange the toy tools under the tree and behind the basket as shown. Rubber cement the small pictures of books onto the garden to look like they are growing in the vegetables. Rubber cement the "lettuce" sign in place in the front part of the garden. Drape Spanish moss on the tree and over the floor.

TITLES:

BEEEE Reading

BEEEE Reading This Summer

Fiction To BEEEE Reading

BACKGROUND: Blue or blue cloud paper

LETTERING: Black four-inch cutouts or die cuts

PROPS: Three large plastic bees; strip of green paper cut to resemble grass; three to five bunches of red tulips, or other silk flowers; T-pins; rubber bands

INSTRUCTIONS: Staple the background to the board. Staple the grass strip across the bottom. Staple the title across the top half of the board, curving the "BEEEE" to simulate the flight of a bee. Put a rubber band around the bee behind the front legs and another in front of the back legs. Then use the bands from the underside of the bee to hook around T-pins stuck into the board. Using this technique, fasten the bees to the board under, over, and at the end of the title.

TITLES:

Hop Into Spring Reading

Hop Into Fiction

Hop Into Reading

BACKGROUND: Zoo, jungle, rainforest, or solid green laminated wrapping paper

LETTERING: Orange four-inch die cuts

FLOORING: Green burlap

PROPS: Tree limbs; large grasshopper; large books; artificial flower bush; green burlap; leaves

INSTRUCTIONS: Staple the background to the showcase walls. Place the tree limb in the showcase. Tape leaves all over the limbs. Drape green burlap around the tree. Stack large books around the showcase floor as shown. Place a large grasshopper on the tree, on top of the books, and one reading an open book by the tree. Add books to the floor of the showcase as desired.

TITLES:

Get In Shape For Spring Training...Read!

Spring Training Reading

Books For Spring Training

BACKGROUND: Blue with clouds; green paper "grass strip"

LETTERING: White three-inch pin backs

FLOORING: Artificial turf

PROPS: Hula hoop; athletic shoes; doll in sports clothes or T-shirt and shorts; hand weights; baseball; books about springtime sports; T-pins; paper grass strip; artificial turf

INSTRUCTIONS: Staple the background to the walls. Staple the "grass" strip across the bottom edges. Put the artificial turf on the floor. Pin the title in the center of the back wall. Hang a hula hoop on a T-pin, framing the title. Hang the shoes by their laces, on another T-pin, next to "Read!" Arrange the books around the floor. Place the doll in the arrangement. Put hand weights and a baseball on and in front of the books.

TITLES:

National Library Week

Cool Reading Cats

Celebrate National Library Week

BACKGROUND: Blue

LETTERING: Banner

FLOORING: Books

PROPS: Stuffed animal; balloons; streamers; books; contest rules sign

INSTRUCTIONS: Students will guess the number of books in the showcase as part of a National Library Week celebration. Staple the background to the showcase walls. Make a banner with the title on it. We used the Print Shop computer program. Staple the banner in the upper one-third of the board. Fill the bottom half of the showcase with books. Staple the contest rules centered under the banner. Place the stuffed animal, streamers, and balloons around the showcase as shown.

TITLES:

Sail Into Reading

Sail Into Fiction

Sail Into Summertime Reading

BACKGROUND: Top two-thirds laminated variegated orange, pink, or yellow tissue paper. Blue for the bottom one-third of the board.

LETTERING: Black four-inch die cuts

PROPS: White paper or fabric; books; poster board; dowel rods; cord or fishing line; hot glue gun

INSTRUCTIONS: Staple the tissue paper background to the top two-thirds of the board, representing a sunset or sunrise. Cut a strip of blue paper with a wavy edge for the bottom third. Staple it to the board. Use slings to hang books in the front in the center of the blue background. Cut a boat shape out of poster board and staple it across the books, as if the books were inside the boat. Cut another strip of "waves" and staple them across the front of the boat. Cut sail shapes from paper or fabric. Glue dowel rods to one sail at right angles. Wedge the upright dowel into the books, forming a mast. Staple the sail to the board. Staple the spinnaker sail to the front portion of the mast and boat. Use fishing line or cord for the lines that anchor the sails.

TITLES:

Sail Into Springtime Reading

Sail Into Reference Skills

Sail Into The Internet

BACKGROUND: Light blue kraft paper

BORDERS: Blue or none

LETTERING: Three-inch pin backs

PROPS: Poster board cutout of a boat; dowel rods for the mast and boom; white cloth or paper for the sail; blue paper; boxes or old books; blue fabric; glue gun

INSTRUCTIONS: Staple the background to the walls. Staple the title to the upper left back wall. Build up the base with boxes and/or books. Cover them with blue fabric. Staple the front (bow) and back (stern) of the boat outline to the wall, bowing it out into a boat shape, and resting the bottom edge on the built-up base. Glue the boom to the mast at a right angle, then glue the sail to the top of the mast, and right and left ends of the boom. Wedge the mast into the base books. Fill the boat with books on boating and/or sailing. Cut the blue paper into a strip a little wider than the width of the showcase opening, with a scalloped "wave" top. Staple the "wave" paper to the side walls and in front of the boat, visually putting the boat into "water."

TITLES:

See Ya Later, Alligator! Iguana Read This Summer?

"Iguana" Read This Year?

"Iguana" Read Science Books?

BACKGROUND: Laminated jungle print wrapping paper

LETTERING: Cartoon "balloons," computer generated and cut into shape

FLOORING: Books or boxes covered with green burlap

PROPS: Tree limb; artificial greenery; Spanish moss; green burlap; toy alligator and iguana (or poster board drawings); books about reptiles; fishing line

INSTRUCTIONS: Staple the background to the walls. Put the tree into place. Attach leaves, vines, and Spanish moss to the tree. Build up the floor with boxes and/or books, then cover with burlap. Tie the iguana onto the tree. Staple "See Ya..." balloon to the wall near the iguana. Put the alligator on the built-up base. Staple "Iguana..." balloon to the wall near the alligator. Arrange books and greenery throughout the scene to create a jungle effect.

TITLES:

"I Do" Plan To Read This Summer

Take A Vow To Read

"I Do" Love Books

BACKGROUND: White

LETTERING: Six-inch pink letters for "I Do" and three-inch black for the rest of the title

FLOORING: White satin

PROPS: Large bride and groom dolls; smaller brides and grooms like Scarlett and Rhett, Barbie and Ken, and various ethnic groups and body types; white tulle material; pink bows; books about weddings; plant stand or books to make a base of varied heights

INSTRUCTIONS: Staple white paper to the walls of the showcase. Build the showcase floor up to three different levels with books or use a three-tiered plant stand. Cover the floor and stand or books with white satin. In the upper left and right corners, hang white tulle drapes with pink bows at the top as shown. Place the bride and groom dolls on the three levels. Some dolls may stand on books. Place wedding planning books and fiction books around and in the white satin as desired.

TITLES:

Electrifying Fiction

Electrifying Reading

Electrifying Books

BACKGROUND: Purple

LETTERING: Laminated aluminum foil four-inch die cuts

PROPS: Poster board; paints; brush; ice pick or awl; chenille craft sticks in various colors; reading list of horror books

INSTRUCTIONS: Staple the background to the board. Draw a large bald head and shoulders the size of the poster board. Color or paint the face. Using a sharp pointed awl or ice pick, punch holes around the outside edge of the top of the head about every one-half inch from ear to ear. Loop colorful craft sticks through each hole and twist back on themselves to fasten. Then bend each craft stick every few inches to make it look like it's standing straight up as illustrated. Staple the face to the lower right quadrant. Staple the title in two arcing lines across the top of the board and upper right quadrant. Staple the reading list in the lower left as shown.

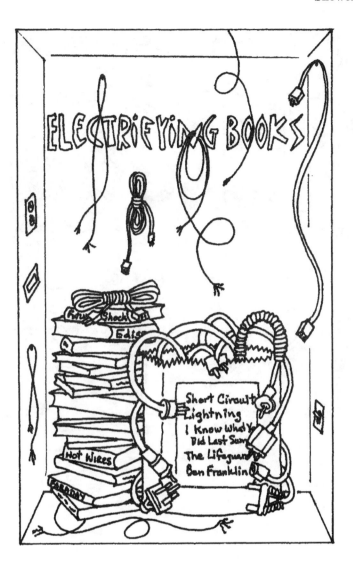

TITLES:

Electrifying Books

Shocking Books

Electrifying Fiction

BACKGROUND: Orange

LETTERING: Computer generated

PROPS: Extension cords; wall outlets; switches; electrical wires; large paper sack; books about electricity, lightning, inventors, and scientists; scary books; connection cables; pushpins; T-pins; reading list; glue; newspapers

INSTRUCTIONS: Staple the background to the walls. Staple the title to the upper back wall. Stack the books on the left side of the floor. Glue the reading list to the front of the sack. Crumple up newspapers and half fill the sack with them. Put the cable connections, extension cords, and wires into the sack, allowing them to spill out and over the top as illustrated. Put the sack on the right side of the floor. Use pushpins and T-pins to hang outlets, switches, and wires from the walls and ceiling of the showcase. Put wires and coiled extension cords on the books and floor as shown.

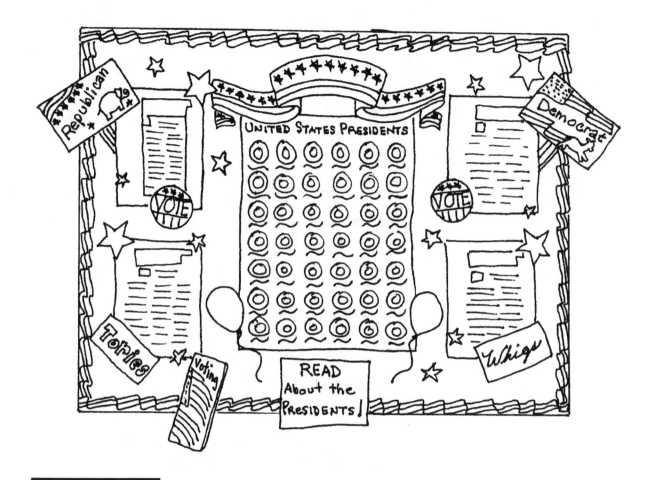

TITLES:

Read About The Presidents

Convention Time Reading

Presidential Reading

BACKGROUND: Red

BORDERS: Purchased red, white, and blue or American flag

LETTERING: Computer-generated sign

PROPS: Poster of all the U.S. presidents; "vote" buttons; balloon punch outs or real balloons; stars; political party signs; elephant cutouts; donkey cutouts; other red, white, and blue memorabilia

INSTRUCTIONS: Staple the background to the board, then staple the border to the edges. Place the title in the upper one-third of the board. Center the presidential poster under the title and attach it to the board. Add historical information about presidential elections. Staple party signs, vote buttons, printouts, stars, balloons, and posters to the board. In election years, post the party platforms and candidate biographies. Use this one in the summer for the political nominating conventions.

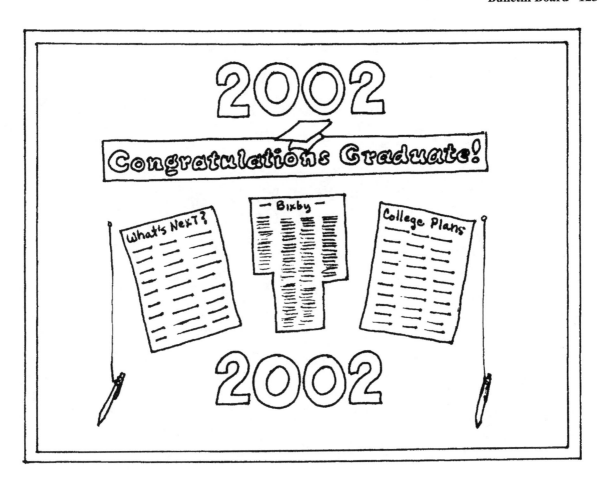

TITLES:

Congratulations Graduate!

Grad Fads

Good-Bye Graduates

BACKGROUND: School colors

LETTERING: Contrasting school color, four-inch cutouts or die cuts; two sets of numbers for the graduation year; purchased banner reading: "Congratulations Graduates" or similar sayings

PROPS: List of graduating seniors (newspaper article, if available); planning sheets labeled "What's Next?" with lines on which the students may write their career plans and "College Plans" with lines to record the college of their choice; two pens; string; pushpins

INSTRUCTIONS: Staple the background to the board. Staple the graduation year, centered, at the top and bottom. Staple the "congratulations" banner, centered, beneath the top year. Staple the class list or article, centered, beneath the banner. Staple the plan sheets on each side of the class list. Tie a string around each ballpoint pen or pencil and hang one from a pushpin beside each list.

Chapter

Lists, Forms, Sources, Suggestions, and Helps

This is the chapter that provides lists, forms, sources, suggestions, and helps. It is hoped that these items will aid the bulletin board and showcase artist in finding and collecting materials to create the boards and showcases featured in this book.

SUPPLY LIST AND SUGGESTED SOURCES

The following lists are suggestions of items that may be used to enhance bulletin boards and showcases. They do not have to be purchased all at once, but start collecting them. The bulletin board and showcase artist may discover alternate ideas and still be able to create the boards and showcases featured in Chapter Three.

Outdoors

twigs and small branches

tree limbs

wood (small logs, stumps)

hay (loose or a large bale)

seashells

rocks (assorted sizes)

leaves

Garage Sales and Home

newspapers

keys

miniature books

dolls (assorted sizes and styles)

carpet scraps (indoor-outdoor and regular)

boxes (assorted sizes)

brown paper sacks

School

opaque projector

laminator

letter-cutting machine

stapler and staples

pushpins

tape (transparent and masking)

Teacher Supply Store

borders (assorted colors and designs)

letters (pin back, cutout)

Posters

from travel agencies

from American Library Association

from book fairs

Craft Stores and Discount Stores

Assorted paper types

kraft

construction

tissue

wrapping

poster board

Party Supplies

streamers
balloons
fans (various sizes and types)
flags (all sizes and countries)
fishnet

Toy Department

garden tools (rake, hoe, shovel)
plastic ducks, insects
dolls on sale

Plants and Leaves

ornamental corn in husks
vines and plants (artificial)
leaves (plastic, paper, fabric, garlands)
Spanish moss

Craft Department

raffia
Styrofoam (cones, circles, sheets, blocks, balls, scraps)
X-ACTO knife
glue gun (preferably hot), glue sticks
pushpins, T-pins, straight pins
cotton batting, stuffing, balls
fabric for backgrounds

Home and Garden Supplies

short section of flower-bed trim (white picket fence)
rope, twine, string, fishing line
dowel rods (assorted sizes)
small pedestal or column
trash bags (black, white, pastels)

Holiday Decorations (watch for postseason sales)

small fir tree
snowflakes (plastic and paper)
assorted artificial pumpkins
tree ornaments

MONTH-BY-MONTH SUGGESTIONS

Using a nine-month format allows planning ahead to keep student interest high. High school upperclassmen ask what next month's display will be. Traffic in the hall by the showcase is buzzing when a new showcase is being installed. The students want to guess or suggest what is being featured. Always listen to their comments. The following list suggests events to be featured each month:

AUGUST

Back To School

Biography As History Month

Book Lovers Day (August 9)

National Aviation Day (August 19)

Romance Awareness Month

Nineteenth Amendment Ratified (women can vote!) August 18, 1920

Romance Books

SEPTEMBER

Back To School

Labor Day (first Monday in September)

National Hispanic Heritage Month (September 15–October 15)

Grandparents Day

Citizenship Day

Fall (around September 22)

Autumnal Equinox

Banned-Book Week (last week of September)

American Indian Day (fourth Friday in September)

Fall Sports

OCTOBER

Autumn

Harvests

National Crime Prevention Month

National Domestic Violence Awareness Month

American Library Association Founded (October 6)

National Children's Day (October 8)

Columbus Day (October 12)

United Nations Day (October 24)

Halloween (October 31)

Mysteries, Horror, and Terror Books

Month-by-Month Suggestions

NOVEMBER

Elections

Veterans Day (November 11)

Native American or National Indian Heritage Month

Harvest Time

National Children's Book Week

Thanksgiving (fourth Thursday in November)

Historical Fiction

Basketball Resumes

DECEMBER

World AIDS Day (December 1)

Holiday Season

Winter Solstice

Winter

Hanukkah

Christmas

Ramadan (December 20–January 17)

Kwanzaa (December 26–January 1)

Winter Sports

JANUARY

New Year's Day

Twelfth Night (January 5)

Epiphany (January 6)

Martin Luther King's Birthday

Science Awareness Month

National Book Month

Robert E. Lee's Birthday (January 19)

Inauguration Day (January 20)

Chinese New Year and Vietnamese New Year (January–February)

FEBRUARY

American Heart Month

American History Month

Black History Month

National Freedom Day (February 1)

Groundhog Day

St. Valentine's Day (February 14)

Future Homemakers of America Week

Future Farmers of America Week

Romance Books

Winter Olympics (every four years)

MARCH

National History Month
Spring
St. Patrick's Day (March 17)
Spring Sports
Women's Studies
Women's History Month
United Nations Day
International Women's Day
Windy Weather
Kites

APRIL

April Fools' Day (April 1)
National Library Week
Rainy Weather
Stormy Weather
Pan American Day (April 14)
National Poetry Month
Pulitzer Prizes Awarded
National Science and Technology Week
Reading Is Fun Week
Earth Day (April 22)
Shakespeare's Birthday (April 23, 1616)
Baseball Resumes

MAY

May Day (May 1)
National Physical Fitness and Sports Month
Cinco de Mayo
V-E Day in Europe (May 8)
Mother's Day (second Sunday in May)
Graduation Day
Armed Forces Day (third Saturday in May)
Memorial Day (last Monday in May)
National Teachers Day (last Monday in May)

JUNE

World History and Culture
Summer Solstice
Summer Reading
Jefferson Davis's Birthday (June 3)

Flag Day (June 14)

Magna Carta Day (signed June 15, 1215)

Father's Day (third Sunday in June)

JULY

Summer Olympics

Independence Day (July 4)

Hot Reads

Celebrate America

Bastille Day in France (July 14)

MONTH   October

YEAR	SHOWCASE	BULLETIN BD #1	BULLETIN BD #2
1994	"Scary Books." Bale of hay, scarecrow, leaves	"Ghost Readers Try the 100's." Ghost buster-type of ghosts	"Spooktacular Media." Kit from Upstart
1995	"Boooks Are Real Treats." Large candy corn, peanut butter kisses, suckers	"Creature Features" poster of werewolf, Dracula, Frankenstein	"Get a life . . . Read." Shar pei poster
1996	"Phantastic Classics." *Phantom of the Opera* memorabilia	"Fall for Books." Leaves, book titles	"Boootiful Books." Ghosts, mysteries
1997	"Spine-Tingling Books." Skeleton reading books under spooky tree	"Wrapped Up in Books." Small skeleton wrapped like a mummy reading	"Notable Books for College-Bound Reading." Music notes
1998	"Sizzling Suspense." Tree, moon, pumpkins, pot of books	"Creature Features." Dracula, Wolfman, Frankenstein, spiders	"Boooks Are Real Treats!" Candy corn, suckers, kisses, mints

Titles from *Bulletin Boards That Capture Them with Pizzazz.* © 1999. Libraries Unlimited

MONTH _____

YEAR	SHOWCASE	BULLETIN BD #1	BULLETIN BD #2

YEAR 2002-2003

MONTH	SHOWCASE	BULLETIN BD #1	BULLETIN BD #2
AUGUST	"Reading Is Timeless." Big Ben	Garfield posters, letters "We're Back!!!"	Mel Gibson; ALA "Read" Poster (which is great hit with faculty)
SEPTEMBER	"Get a Kick Out of Reading." Pillow person, soccer	"Kick Off the Year to a Good Start with Reading." Shoe and leg	"What are you cut out to be??" paper dolls
OCTOBER	"Sizzling Suspense." Tree, moon, pumpkins, pot of books	"Creature Features." Dracula, Wolfman, Frankenstein	"Boooks Are Real Treats." Candy corn, suckers, peppermints
NOVEMBER	"Give Thanks for Books." Critters read around log and stumps	"Rake in a Good Book." Rake and leaves, basket	"Tree-mendous Fall Reading." Tree, leaves
DECEMBER	"Present the Joy of Reading." Santa reads to animals	"Give the Gift of Reading." Reindeer head, present	"Wrapped Up in Reading." Packages, ribbons
JANUARY	"Winterize with Reading." Auto info snow scene, dolls	"Read in the New Year." Polar bear and party hats, etc.	"Snow Time Is Book Time." Snowman
FEBRUARY	"Read to Your Sweetheart." Gorillas and monkeys	"Sweet Heart Reading." Valentine candy box	"Devoted Dog Tales." Fake fur, Scottie
MARCH	"Swing into Spring Reading." Bats, golf clubs, racquets	"Debug Your Brain: Read!" Ladybugs	"Big Hits." Baseballs and players, Styrofoam balls
APRIL	"Stormy Weather Reading." Tornado, raindrops, safety tips	"April Showers Bring Reading Hours." Umbrella	"Libraries Are the Keys to Your Future." Keys
MAY	"Get Hooked on Reading." Stuffed fish, lures, etc.	"Congratulations Graduates." Mortar boards, grad year	"Rare Books." Paper plates, red-and-white-checked tablecloth
JUNE	"Fan-tastic Books for Summer." Fans' lists of books	"Cool Cats Read." Rock-and-roll cat, puppet	"Stay Cool This Summer: Read!" Pillow person, sand
JULY	"Gold Medal Reading." Feature Olympics	"Book an Adventure in Australia." Koala bears	"Hot Reading." Stove, pots and pans

Titles from *Bulletin Boards That Capture Them with Pizzazz.* © 1999. Libraries Unlimited

YEAR _____

MONTH	SHOWCASE	BULLETIN BD #1	BULLETIN BD #2
AUGUST			
SEPTEMBER			
OCTOBER			
NOVEMBER			
DECEMBER			
JANUARY			
FEBRUARY			
MARCH			
APRIL			
MAY			
JUNE			
JULY			

BIBLIOGRAPHY

Hatch, Jane M. *The American Book of Days*. New York: H. W. Wilson, 1978.

Microsoft Encarta '95 Electronic Encyclopedia, 1995 edition, CD-ROM.

SOURCES FOR IDEAS AND SUPPLIES

ALA Graphics
American Library Association
50 E. Huron Street
Chicago, IL 60611
www.alastore.ala.org (ALA online store)

Demco
P.O. Box 7488
Madison, WI 53707-7488

Upstart
W5527 Highway 106
P.O. Box 800M
Fort Atkinson, WI 53538-0800

Index

"B" after the page number indicates bulletin boards; "S" indicates showcases